We Live Forever

A STUDY OF LIFE AFTER DEATH

By
Lehman Strauss

LOIZEAUX BROTHERS
Neptune, New Jersey

FIRST EDITION, 1947
SEVENTH PRINTING, DECEMBER 1976

ISBN 0-87213-830-5

PRINTED IN THE UNITED STATES OF AMERICA

To my dear Father and Mother

Joseph and Pearl L. Strauss

always understanding, gracious and considerate of their children.

INTRODUCTION

By Dr. William Culbertson

Dean, Moody Bible Institute

Undoubtedly the greatest joy of the Christian teacher is to see his former students "walking in the truth." The great goal of all spiritual instruction is the transformation of life which results from knowing God. There is one joy that the Christian teacher may have in addition, and while it is secondary to the one mentioned above, it is nevertheless thrilling and real: it is the joy of seeing the former pupil used of God in instructing others. In limited measure it has been my privilege in days past to instruct my brother, the author of this book. Pastor Lehman Strauss thus fulfills the joys just mentioned.

It is a genuine pleasure to write this word of introduction to this volume. Whatever disagreement there may be on incidental statements in this volume, all evangelicals will rejoice in the clear, positive, scriptural treatment on that part of eschatology which deals with death and resurrection, with heaven and hell. This word is rigidly Biblical, lovingly evangelistic, and tenderly comforting. May God greatly bless this book as my brother in Christ teaches others also.

William Culbertson

PREFACE

The chapters in this little book are not intended for scholars and exegetes. They were written to help the average Christian and to show the way of salvation to any unbelievers into whose hands they might come.

No claim to originality is made in behalf of the contents. Material has been gathered from many sources, and quotations are made from others because the writer of this book feels that they have given better expression to what he wanted to say.

The galley proof of this book was read in whole by Dr. William Culbertson, the beloved Dean of the Moody Bible Institute. As a result of his kind and constructive criticism, some changes have been made. Whatever the defects of the book, they would have been more numerous apart from his suggestions.

The author wishes to acknowledge with thanks the faithfulness of the Misses Evelyn Den Bleyker and Helen Hertzler, and Mr. Francis V. Toppin, members of the Calvary Baptist Church of Bristol, Pennsylvania in helping to prepare the manuscript for publication.

CONTENTS

CHAPTER ONE

DEATH

"And as it is appointed unto men once to die, but after this the judgment" (Hebrews 9:27).

"IN the day that thou eatest thereof thou shalt surely die" (Genesis 2:17). "There shall be no more death" (Revelation 21:4). Between these two statements in the Scripture lie all the efforts of science to increase the life span, the consummation of civilization, the endeavors to build a better world, and all the joys and sorrows of billions of individuals that eternity alone has the record of. Hidden between the covers of this record book is the story of the whole human race cursed by the fall of the first parent Adam. The surging, aimless mass of lost humanity has been impelled by fear—fear of the dark, fear of disease, fear of the supernatural, fear of the unknown, fear of death. The fear of death is but the apogee of all fears. Men avoid it, hate it, fight against it. The undertaker uses every artificial means at his disposal to cover the fact of it. Yet the fact of death remains and will remain until that day when, through the glorious power of Christ who was triumphant over death, the scroll of heaven will be rolled back, the saints of God shall enjoy the blissful ages of eternity, and "there shall be no more death."

THE CERTAINTY OF DEATH

The valley of the shadow of death is the longest valley in the world. It began with Adam and has continued through six thousand years of human history. Men like to postpone that dreadful moment when they must pass through the dark valley, but death underscores each life and refuses to accept the person of any man. Death does not take into account whether we have been profitable or detrimental to society. Every step that we take brings us nearer to the grave, and it is but a matter of time until we must bid farewell to every earthly tie. With all of the wisdom of the medical profession and the use of scientific discoveries, we must agree with the wise preacher of old who said: "For the living know that they shall die" (Ecclesiastes 9:5).

The Bible contains much warning about death, speaking as frequently on this subject as it does about any other. In the garden of Eden where death had never entered, Adam and Eve were instructd by God to refrain from the forbidden fruit with the accompanying warning:

> "In the day that thou eatest thereof thou shalt surely *die*" (Genesis 2:17).

We know that they did eat; and at the very moment the judgment of God passed upon them, their bodies commenced the process of death and decay. "And all the days that Adam lived were nine hundred and thirty years: *and he died*" (Genesis 5:5).

On one page of our Bible we have the genealogy from Adam to Noah; and with only one exception, Enoch, the man who walked with God and was translated, the refrain is repeated—*"And he died."*

> "'And all the days of Seth were nine hundred and twelve years: *and he died*" (Genesis 5:8).
> "And all the days of Enos were nine hundred and five years: *and he died*" (Genesis 5:11).
> "And all the days of Cainan were nine hundred and ten years: *and he died*" (Genesis 5:14).
> "And all the days of Mahalaleel were eight hundred ninety and five years: *and he died*" (Genesis 5:17).
> "And all the days of Jared were nine hundred sixty and two years: *and he died*" (Genesis 5:20).
> "And all the days of Methuselah were nine hundred sixty and nine years: *and he died*" (Genesis 5:27).

"And all the days of Lamech were seven hundred
seventy and seven years: *and he died*" (Genesis 5:31).

The Patriarchs, Prophets, and Apostles did not hesi-
tate to declare that death is certain. Noah preached
righteousness and the judgment of God. He warned
men that if they would not repent, the Lord would
destroy them from the face of the earth (Genesis 6:7).
Men only mocked at the old preacher's sermon, and
then God struck the whole earth with death and
destruction. The divine record has it that the waters
prevailed for forty days on the earth until every hill
was covered. And then we read:

> "*And all flesh died* that moved upon the earth,
> both of fowl, and of cattle, and of beast, and of
> every creeping thing that creepeth upon the
> earth, *and every man*" (Genesis 7:21).

Abraham faced the grim reality of death when he
offered Isaac as a sacrifice to the Lord. Though Isaac
was spared, a ram died in his stead. Then we read:
"*And Sarah died*" (Genesis 23:2).

> "And the Lord said unto Moses, Behold, thy days
> approach that thou must *die*" (Deuteronomy 31:14).
> Isaiah said to Hezekiah: "Set thine house in order;
> for thou shalt *die*, and not live" (2 Kings 20:1).
> Jeremiah warned Hananiah: "This year thou shalt
> *die*" (Jeremiah 28:16).
> Ezekiel preached the Word of the Lord: "The
> soul that sinneth, it shall *die*" (Ezekiel 18:4).
> "That wicked man shall *die* in his iniquity"
> (Ezekiel 33:8).

When Jesus told the story of the rich man and
Lazarus, He said:

> "The beggar *died* . . . The rich man also *died*"
> (Luke 16:22).

When Christ was brought before the multitude, the Jews said:

> "We have a law, and by our law He ought to *die*"
> (John 19:7).

Of Dorcas, Luke writes:
> "She was sick, and *died*" (Acts 9:37).

How full the Bible is of the subject of death! We cannot study the life of any Bible character, save Enoch and Elijah, without being reminded that they all died. Life insurance companies become rich simply by pointing out that all men must die, and the agents have little difficulty in selling a policy by merely stating that death may come suddenly and unexpectedly. Any undertaker who conducts a respectable business is assured of a comfortable living with those values that money can buy. Even architects and builders take death into account when they plan a structure. Dr. John Rice tells that when his congregation in Dallas was preparing plans for a new church building the architect insisted on discussing the stairways, for, said he: "One rule we architects try to remember is that every stairway and every bedroom door must be large enough to admit a coffin!"

According to *Life* magazine, William Randolph Hearst is seventy-five years of age, and "in his presence it is forbidden to mention death". However, just recently when yielding voting control of his publications to an attorney, "the man who has arrogantly and brilliantly ruled a $200,000,000 empire acknowledged death although he did not mention it". The statement merely read that Mr. Hearst had become "conscious of the uncertainties of life". We admit that death is an unpleasant subject. Yet no man can rule it out of his future. Refusing to talk or to think about death does not alter the fact of death. We call our cemeteries "memorial parks". Still they are the abode of the dead.

The Bible speaks of

> "The law of sin and *death* (Romans 8:2).

The Apostle Paul says:

> "We had the sentence of *death* in ourselves"
> (2 Corinthians 1:9).
> "So then *death* worketh in us" (2 Corinthians 4:12).

The Epistle to the Hebrews speaks of men

> "Who through fear of *death* were all their lifetime subject to bondage" (Hebrews 2:15).

There is no escaping death. Try as hard as we can, the rider on the pale horse will pay his visit to each of us. He is blind to all tears and deaf to all prayers and pleadings. He must come to us, for he is sent by *appointment*. "It is *appointed* unto men once to die". It is the judgment of the Almighty, it is by divine *appointment*. The death-bed, the crepe, the funeral, the grave, and the broken-hearted sighs and tears of the bereaved all tell us that "man *dieth*".

THE CAUSE OF DEATH

Where did death originate? We acknowledge the sovereignty of God, but must we accept the theory that every event of man's life, including the manner and time of his death were minutely fixed by God before creation? We answer that we can find no sound basis for such a dogmatic view. (God is sovereign to be certain, but He created man a free agent with the will to decide for himself. In his primitive state in the Garden of Eden, man had never seen anyone die. He never looked on while another gasped for breath and failed to find it.)

The first time that the subject of death is mentioned in the Bible it is given as a warning to our first parents. There man in his primitive state was enjoying blissful communion with God.

> "And the LORD God commanded the man, saying, Of every tree of the garden thou mayest freely eat: But of the tree of the knowledge of good and evil, thou shalt not eat of it: for in the day that thou eatest thereof *thou shalt surely die*" (Genesis 2:16, 17).

Adam knew that he was alive, but he was a stranger to the subject of death until he heard this word from the Lord. Now he is on his own. He has a knowledge of what is right and what is wrong. He knows that to obey God will mean continuous and unending life and to disobey will bring the sentence of death. The power of choice and the right to decide is now left with man. However, Satan would not allow the situation to go unchallenged. Though he taunted and tempted Eve he could not *force* her to eat the fruit. Both she and her husband partook of it by their own *choice,* and in so doing they incurred the displeasure of the Lord. The warning He gave was plain: "In the day that thou eatest thereof thou shalt surely die". Being holy and righteous in all of His judgments, God could do nothing other than pass the sentence of death. Hence Adam listened to what the consequences of his own wrong-doing had brought upon himself—

> "In the sweat of thy face shalt thou eat bread, till thou return unto the ground; for out of it wast thou taken: for dust thou art, and unto dust shalt thou return" (Genesis 3:19).

God never acts in judgment nor does He allow anything to come to pass unless there is a just cause. So when He pronounced death upon the human race it was because Adam and Eve had disobeyed God and turned from the truth. Though the warning of the Lord had come in soundness and simplicity man chose to sin, knowing all the while that it meant death. Man cannot plead innocency on the ground of the sovereignty of God. He is appointed to die because he has transgressed the Law of God, and the Lord's justice in the sentence of death is so undeniable that every mouth is stopped and all the world is guilty before Him. Man can offer no legitimate reason why the death sentence should not have been passed, for

> "The wages of sin is death" (Romans 6:23).
> "The soul that sinneth, it shall die" (Ezekiel 18:4).
> "Sin, when it is finished, bringeth forth death" (James 1:15).
> "By one man sin entered into the world, and death by sin" (Romans 5:12).
> "So then death worketh in us" (2 Corinthians 4:12).
> "For all have sinned" (Romans 3:23).

Every time that death strikes and a loved one is suddenly taken away, it is as if we hear the cachinnation of sin and Satan. Sin plays with man for a time just as a cat plays with a mouse. Sin will allow us to run here and there, to pursue happiness, worldly pleasure and power; but the game of life is brief. In the end sin has tracked down each of us, and each pays with his life. Inasmuch as "all have sinned" (Romans 3:23), we search in vain in our efforts to discover the secret of victory over death, for "What man is he that liveth, and shall not see death?" (Psalm 89:48).

Death is still in our midst holding the whole world in fear and subjection. The reason men shrink from it is because "the sting of death is sin" (1 Corinthians

15:56). Because our nature is sinful and our hearts
wicked, death continues to prick us and drive us
toward the grave as the goad drives an ox to slaughter.
Jesus said that ours is a wicked and an adulterous age.
Until Christ comes back with His Church to rule the
earth, "the last enemy that shall be destroyed is death"
(1 Corinthians 15:26). Even to the end of the millennium death will hold within its grasp all the wicked
dead. Until Satan and all unbelievers are cast into the
lake of fire, death will have a vise-like grip upon sinners. But how comforting and consoling for the
Christian when he looks for Him, even our blessed
Lord Jesus who, when He comes the second time with
His own, will subdue all things, even the power of
death!

THE COURSE OF DEATH

Death does not affect all men in the same way simply
because it does not lead all men in the same direction.
We realize that here we are assuming that death is not
the consummation of all existence. Furthermore we
are aware of the fact that there are a great many people
in the world today who do not believe in an existing
consciousness after death. Only recently I talked with
a gentleman who believes that death is the cessation of
man's existence. He compared the death of man to a
leaf falling from a tree in October. Disregarding the
positive proof of immortality, we will content ourselves
with a brief consideration of one of two courses that
death must take.

In one hospital ward two patients may die at
exactly the same moment. While the root cause of
these deaths may be the same in each case, the dying
of one can be something altogether different from
the dying of the other. We have seen how that death
was the only real satisfaction for sin. It was the only

punishment for sin that could satisfy the righteous demands of God. Since all men, who were at one time in the loins of Adam, possess Adam's fallen nature, it stands that all must die the physical death of the body. However, as Abraham Kuyper has said: "In the valley of the shadow of death, the great highway on which people walk divides itself, and continues on one side upward unto eternal life, and on the other with a declining path downward into eternal death".

We can understand this only as we know something of the true purpose of the death of Jesus Christ. Since sin must be punished by death, Jesus went to the cross and died as the punishment for sin and thus at the same time offered Himself as the satisfaction for sin. Peter declares that "Christ also hath once suffered for sins, the just for the unjust, that He might bring us to God, being put to death in the flesh" (1 Peter 3:18). Here we are told that Christ was put to death for sins "that He might bring us to God". Those who fall asleep in the Lord take the upward course to Heaven and to God. Having accepted Jesus Christ as their Sin-Bearer and Saviour from sin, they are brought to God by virtue of His sacrificial and vicarious death. Believers are able to say: "The Lord hath laid on Him the iniquity of us all" (Isaiah 53:6). As Jesus hung dying upon the Cross, He was the true sin-offering for His people. We were, by nature, on the downward course, doomed to be separated from God; but Jesus, by virtue of His death, provided a new destiny. Dr. Harry Rimmer has said: "When Jesus died to change the trend of human thought, He also died to change the road of human history. Through a false philosophy, mankind was pursuing a fatal destiny. The impact of the cross bent human history out of the course in which it was flowing, and directed mankind toward God." Whenever a true believer dies he is said to have fallen "asleep" (1 Thessalonians 4:13, 15; 1 Corinthians 15:6), and immediately his soul takes the upward course to be with the Lord.

But what course does death pursue in the case of an unbeliever? We have already stated that the only other course remaining is the declining path into eternal death. Once again we must make an assumption, that of belief in a literal place of endless torment for all who reject the atoning work of Christ when He died on Calvary's Cross.

Since the death of Christ paid for the believer the punishment of sin, and death to him is a pleasant ascension into the Father's presence, it follows that the death of the unbeliever is an unpleasant descent away from the presence of God. When the unbeliever gives up the ghost, breathing his last breath, he passes from this world into a spiritual and eternal death and Hell. Both are conscious, but death was forced to pursue a different course for each. Both the rich man and Lazarus died in the story told by our Lord. Lazarus was carried into Abraham's bosom while the rich man was sent to Hell (Luke 16:19-24).

Dear Reader, where are you? Yes, you are still alive in this world; but remember, death is slowly but surely overtaking you. Soon you must say farewell to every earthly tie and enter into an endless eternity. Since Christ died to bring you to God, it is self-evident that you are far from God, and unprepared and unfit for Heaven. Will you trust the Saviour now? "He that believeth not shall be damned" (Mark 16:16).

CHAPTER TWO

MAN A TRINITY—SPIRIT, SOUL, BODY

THE Christian doctrine of immortality cannot be understood apart from the right conception of the tripartite nature of men. Many think that man is a physical being only. There is a great danger of any man thinking thus of himself. In his desire to satisfy the needs of the body there is the tendency on man's part to lose sight of the fact that he is immortal. There have been persons who have lived all of their lives either in ignorance or willful neglect of a life after death, but upon their death-bed they suddenly realized that they were more than physical beings.

There is an idea also that prevails largely today that man consists of only two component parts; namely, body and spirit. In the thinking of the writer this view appears to be one that might create confusion in the minds of many Christians. While soul and spirit are so closely related that it is sometimes difficult to distinguish accurately between them, there seems to be only one logical conclusion; namely, that "soul" and "spirit" are not the same. The Bible does make a distinction.

Man is a triune being because he is created in the image of God. "God said, Let us make man in Our image" (Genesis 1:26). We know that God is a Trinity. The Holy Trinity is clearly set forth in the Apostle Paul's benediction that closed his Second Corinthian Epistle: "The grace of the *Lord Jesus Christ*, and the love of *God*, and the communion of the *Holy Ghost*, be with you all. Amen" (2 Corinthians 13:14). Our Lord Himself said, in what we call "The Great Commission: "Go ye therefore, and teach all nations, baptizing them in the name of the *Father*, and of the *Son*, and of the *Holy Ghost*" (Matthew 28:19). Created in the image of God, man is likewise a trinity. He has a spiritual nature that is separate and distinct from the body in which it dwells.

The two following passages from the Bible clearly establish the fact that man is a triune being composed of spirit, soul, and body—

> "I pray God your whole *spirit* and *soul* and *body* be preserved blameless unto the coming of our Lord Jesus Christ" (1 Thessalonians 5:23).

> "For the word of God is quick, and powerful, and sharper than any two edged sword, piercing even to the dividing asunder of *soul* and *spirit*, and of the *joints* and *marrow* (body), and is a discerner of the thoughts and intents of the heart" (Hebrews 4:12).

In spite of the erroneous teaching of "Jehovah's Witnesses" and of other false sects that "no man has a soul", the Bible states emphatically that man was created a trinity of spirit, soul, and body even as the eternal God is Himself a trinity of Father, Son, and Holy Ghost. The trinity of man is an essential part of the image relationship between him and God. Life is not ultimately physical and the body is not the whole man. And we might add that neither the body in itself, nor the soul in itself, nor the spirit in itself makes up the whole man, but he is "spirit and soul and body". This must be seriously considered and definitely agreed to before we can comprehend with any accuracy the subject of life after death. In this opening chapter we shall confine our material to the spirit and the soul inasmuch as the body will be considered in succeeding chapters on the resurrection.

The Spirit

The word "spirit" when used in the Scriptures has several meanings. Whenever the word "Spirit" appears used with a capital letter, it has but one meaning. It is the name of the third Person of the Trinity, the Holy Spirit of God. The word "spirit" spelled with a small letter may have one of several different meanings. It can have direct reference to the spirit of man which is as much a part of the tripartite nature of man as the Spirit of the living God is a Person of the Holy Trinity. Or it can indicate an evil spirit such as any agent of the Devil. We will confine ourselves here to the Biblical usage of the word only as it relates to the spirit of man, one of the three constituent parts of his being.

The threefold nature of man might be illustrated in several ways. Dr. Clarence Larkin uses three circles (*"Rightly Dividing The Word"*, page 86). The outer circle stands for the *body* of man, the middle circle for the *soul*, and the inner for the *spirit*. At this point it will be well to quote a portion from Dr. Larkin's book:

> "In the outer circle the 'Body' is shown as touching the Material world through the five senses of 'Sight', 'Smell', 'Hearing', 'Taste' and 'Touch'.

> "The Gates to the 'Soul' are 'Imagination', 'Conscience', 'Memory', 'Reason' and the 'Affections'.

> "The 'Spirit' receives impressions of outward and material things through the Soul. The spiritual faculties of the 'Spirit' are 'Faith', 'Hope', 'Reverence', 'Prayer' and 'Worship'.

> "In his unfallen state the 'Spirit' of man was
> illuminated from Heaven, but when the human
> race fell in Adam, sin closed the window of the
> Spirit, pulled down the curtain, and the cham-
> ber of the spirit became a death chamber, and
> remains so in every unregenerate heart, until
> the Life and Light giving power of the Holy
> Spirit floods that chamber with the life and
> Light giving power of the new life in Christ
> Jesus."

It develops then that the spirit of man, being the
sphere of God-consciousness, is the inner or private
office of man where the work of regeneration takes
place. Dr. James R. Graham says that the main theatre
of the Holy Spirit's activity in man, and the part of
man's nature with which He has peculiar affinity, is
the spirit of man. The Apostle Paul gives us the Word
of God on this, a passage that is sadly neglected. Quoting from the sixty-fourth chapter of the book of the
Prophet Isaiah, Paul wrote:

> "But as it is written, Eye hath not seen, nor
> ear heard, neither have entered into the heart
> of man, the things which God hath prepared for
> them that love Him."

A great many people stop here, content to remain in
ignorance. However, Paul continues:

> "But God hath revealed them unto us by His
> Spirit: for the Spirit searcheth all things, yea,
> the deep things of God.
>
> "For what man knoweth the things of a man,
> save the spirit of man which is in him? even so
> the things of God knoweth no man, but the
> Spirit of God" (1 Corinthians 2:9-11).

Man in his unregenerate state comes to know the
things of man by the operation of "the spirit of man"

which is in him. If I have a will to know certain scientific facts, by my human spirit I am enabled to investigate, think, and weigh evidence. If I set myself to the task, I may become a scientist of world-reknown and of great accomplishments. However, my human spirit is "limited to the things of man." If I want to know about the things of God, my dead and dormant spirit is not able to know them—

> "The natural man receiveth not the things of the Spirit of God: for they are foolishness unto him: neither can he know them, because they are spiritually discerned" (1Corinthians 2:14).

The human spirit requires "the spark of regeneration" before there is an understanding of the things of God. Man's spiritual nature must be renewed before there is a true conception of Godliness. Only one thing stands as a guard at the door of man's spirit, and that is his own *will*. When the will is surrendered, the Holy Spirit takes up His abode in the spirit of man. And when that transaction takes place we will know it, for, says Paul:

> "The Spirit Himself (meaning the Holy Spirit) beareth witness with our spirit, that we are children of God" (Romans 8:16 R. V.).

Many people confess that they get nothing out of the Bible even though they attend church and read their Bibles regularly. Perhaps they do not know that they are not regenerated and that they need to yield their will to the Spirit of God so that He can renew their human spirits. The deep things of God never will be understood by the world outside of Jesus Christ. Our Lord warned His disciples,

"Give not that which is holy unto the dogs, neither cast ye your pearls before swine" (Matthew 7:6).

The spirit of the unregenerate man has no more capacity to appreciate the things of God than a dog has to appreciate holy things, or a hog a genuine pearl necklace. We read that "The dog is turned to his own vomit again; and the sow that was washed to her wallowing in the mire" (2 Peter 2:22). This they did because the dog was a dog and the sow was a sow. No amount of religion or church activity can change the spirit of the unregenerate man. "Remember", says Dr. G. Campbell Morgan, "if out of false charity or pity you allow men of material ideals and worldly wisdom to touch holy things, to handle the pearls of the Kingdom, presently they will turn and rend you. That is the whole history of Christendom's ruin, in the measure in which Christendom is ruined. We gave holy things to dogs. We cast the pearls of the Kingdom before swine". The ministry of Christ's Church dare not be entrusted to any man who has not been born again, for "That which is born of the flesh is flesh; and that which is born of the Spirit is spirit" (John 3:6).

The Bible says: "There is a spirit in man: and the inspiration of the Almighty giveth them understanding" (Job 32:8). Here we are told that it is the spirit of man that is given understanding. The materialist tells us that the spirit of man is the air that he breathes, and that man's body is all there is to his personality. Such is not the case. The spirit of man is his personality and it is that which differentiates him from the lower animal creation. If "spirit" meant merely "breath", God certainly would not deal with it as a personality. He is called "The God of the spirits of all flesh" (Numbers 16:22), and "the Father of spirits" (Hebrews 12:9). It is by his spirit that the

Christian both serves and worships God. Paul testified: "For God is my witness, Whom I serve with my *spirit* in the Gospel" (Romans 1:9). Jesus said: "God is a spirit: and they that worship Him must worship Him in *spirit* and in truth" (John 4:24).

THE SOUL

Man not only has a living soul but he *is* a living soul. The Bible says: "And the Lord God formed man of the dust of the ground, and breathed into his nostrils the breath of life, and man became a living soul" (Genesis 2:7). We must be careful not to confound that which is truly spiritual and that which is merely soulish or psychical. We have seen that the spirit of man is the sphere of activity where the Holy Spirit operates in regeneration. Just so is the soul the sphere of activity where Satan operates making his appeal to the affections and emotions of man.

Satan knows full well that he dominates the psychical or the soulish man. Therefore he does not care if a man goes to a church where the Spirit of God is not in evidence. He knows that his victim is a creature of emotions, and it matters not if the emotions are stirred to sentimentalism or even to tears, just so long as man's spirit does not come in contact with God's Holy Spirit. Personally, I believe that Satan would rather have man go to a modernistic church where there is false worship than he would have him go to a house of prostitution. The soul is the seat of the passions, the feelings, and the desires of man; and Satan is satisfied if he can master these. F. W. Grant has said that the soul is the seat of the affections, right or wrong, of love, hate, lusts, and even the appetites of the body.

Hamor said to Jacob, "The soul of my son Schechem longeth for your daughter" (Genesis 34:8).

Of David and Jonathan it is written: "The soul of Jonathan was knit with the soul of David, and Jonathan loved him as his own soul" (1 Samuel 18:1). These passages show the soul to be the seat of the affections.

But as the soul loves, so it also hates. We read of those "that are hated of David's soul" (2 Samuel 5:8).

It is in the soul where fleshly lusts, desires, and appetites arise—

> "Abstain from fleshly lusts which war against the soul" (1 Peter 2:11).
>
> "As cold waters to a thirsty soul, so is good news from a far country" (Proverbs 25:25).
>
> "It shall be even as when a hungry man dreameth, and behold, he eateth; but he awaketh, and his soul is empty: or as when a thirsty man dreameth, and, behold, he drinketh; but he awaketh, and, behold, he is faint, and *his soul hath appetite*" (Isaiah 29:8).

The soul of man, that is, his affections and desires, are never directed Godward until after the spirit has become regenerated. Man can never love God nor the things of God until he is born from above. He may have a troubled conscience or be so stirred emotionally that he may weep bitterly, and still remain dead in trespasses and in sins. We do not feel that we are guilty of judging men when we state that some who have answered an altar call and shed tears never were born again. Man's desires and affections are turned toward God when he realizes his sinful condition and God's grace in salvation. When the Spirit of God illuminates the spirit of a man with divine light and life, that man begins to yield his affections and faculties to God.

The Virgin Mary said: "My soul doth magnify the Lord, And my spirit hath rejoiced in God my Saviour"

(Luke 1:46, 47). She could not extol the Lord in her soul until she had recognized God in her spirit as her Saviour. The initial triumph is in the spirit when Jesus Christ is acknowledged as personal Saviour.

In that immortal classic of the Psalms, David says: "He restoreth my soul" (Psalm 23:3). The Hebrew word translated "restoreth" is said to mean quite literally "turneth back". At no time had David lost his salvation, but there were times when his affections and desires were turned from the Lord, as in the case of his sin with Bathsheba. Having become one of the Divine Shepherd's flock, he testified: "The Lord turneth back my soul". The Christian who is enjoying unbroken communion with his Lord will then be able to say, "Bless the Lord, O my soul: and all that is within me, bless His holy name" (Psalm 103:1).

CHAPTER THREE

CAN WE BELIEVE IN IMMORTALITY?

THE word immortal means exemption from liability to death. That which is immortal is not liable to death. History shows that wherever man has appeared there has been the idea of a longer span of life than that between the cradle and the grave. Only a few have dared to believe that death ends all and that with the death of the body there is the death of the spirit and soul of man. But God have mercy on us if the grave marks our end! "If in this life only we have hope in Christ, we are of all men most miserable" (1 Corinthians 15:19). And certainly there is naught but misery and despair in the words of the agnostic who said:

> "There is one steady star: and dim from afar,
> Comes the solace that dies in its gleam;
> There's the coffin nail's rust; the brain in
>   white dust;
> And the sleeping that knows no dream."

This song of unbelief says there is a "sleeping that knows no dream." Contrariwise, the Apostle Paul by the Holy Spirit says: "We know that if our earthly house of this tabernacle were dissolved, we have a building of God, an house not made with hands, eternal in the heavens" (2 Corinthians 5:1).

THE WITNESS OF THE ANCIENTS

Wherever death has come it seems to have brought with it a conscious assurance of immortality. The immortal soul of saint and savage alike has voiced a hope in life beyond the grave. The idea of the permanency of death seldom was entertained in the mind of man.

Egypt, the classroom of the world's finest arts and sciences, had a strong faith and a feeling of certainty in immortality. Professor Salmond in his "Doctrine of Immortality" says that the Egyptians had the reputation of being the first people who taught the doctrine of immortality. Very often the coffin was referred to as "the chest of the living". The Egyptian art of embalming grew out of their belief in immortality. Their conception of a future life originated the idea and construction of the pyramids, one of the wonders of the world. These huge monuments were erected because it was believed that the soul returned to the body and required an eternal abode. So the mighty pyramids and Egyptian mummies tell us of the ancient belief in a deathless soul.

The heathen of Africa believe in life after death. We are told that the wives of the deceased take up their residence near the tomb so that they can remain the rest of their earthly lives "to watch the departed spirit". Madison C. Peters quotes David Livingstone's story of his travels in which Livingstone tells of the belief of old Chinsunse: "We live only a few days here, but we live again after death; we do not know where, or in what condition, or with what companions, for the dead never return to tell us. Sometimes the dead do come back and appear to us in our dreams; but they never speak, nor tell us where they have gone, nor how they fare." Only recently we listened to testimonies of returned missionaries, relating the belief of the African in life after death.

Steeped in savagery, the Indian of other lands as well as those in North America, had some idea of a future life. In some ancient Asiatic tribes the belief was held that the next world could be reached by the cremation of the body, the fire god taking the deceased to the gods of the other world. Sometimes animals were sacrificed in the fire to precede the corpse to the land beyond. Some North American Indians, believing that they were providing their departed tribesman with the necessary equipment for the land where the Great Spirit lives, buried their dead with bow and arrow and canoe. The Indians had many and various customs of expressing their belief in a life beyond the grave. When a Seneca Indian maiden died a young bird was imprisoned until it first learned how to sing. It was then given messages of affection and loosed over the grave of the maiden in the belief that it would neither close its eyes nor fold its wings until it had flown to the spirit-world and delivered the message of love to her who had died.

Through six millenniums of human history man has looked upon immortality as a reality. Universally believed, it is the most indestructible of all instincts and the most penetrating of all intuitions. We agree with Dr. Lockyer when he said: "Without hesitation, affirm that the belief in a future state was derived from a revelation made to our first parents by their Creator, and that it travelled down the ages. The Hope of Immortality, resident within the breast of both savages and saints, was planted there by Him who has no beginning or end."

THE WITNESS OF THE BIBLE

When we approach the Bible on the subject of immortality, it is well to have in mind a few important facts that are basic and necessary to a proper understanding of the subject. Nowhere in the Bible is the expression to be found, "the immortality of the soul." Nor is there written anything about "the immortal soul." We are not suggesting for a moment that Scripture teaches anything about the sleep or annihilation of the soul at death. The thought of the soul's endless being is true enough, but it is not Scriptural language to refer to "the immortality of the soul." The Word of God assumes the eternal existence of every soul regardless of its destiny. Every man's soul is immortal and can never be annihilated. Jesus said: "Fear not them which kill the body, but are not able to kill the soul: but rather fear him which is able to destroy both soul and body in Hell" (Matt. 10:28). Now those who teach "soul-sleep" would have us believe that their doctrine is Biblical, when actually they have falsified the facts by their misinterpretation of Scripture. Man can kill the body, but that is the worst he can do. God alone can take hold of both body and soul and condemn them.

THREE KINDS OF DEATH

It is true we read: "The soul that sinneth, it shall die" (Ezekiel 18:4), but neither here nor elsewhere in Scripture does a reference to the soul dying mean a state of non-existence, or even one of unconsciousness. The Bible teaches that there are three kinds of death and it distinguishs clearly between each. First, there is physical death, or the separation of the soul from the body. This is the death of the body to which reference was made in Hebrews 9:27, "It is appointed unto men once to die". Second, the Bible teaches that there is a spiritual death. This is the separation of the soul from God, the condition of all unbelievers of whom Paul says they are "dead in trespasses and sins" (Ephesians 2:1), and "alienated from the life of God" (Ephesians 4:18). Third, there is eternal death or banishment from God. All who suffer eternal death are conscious, but "shall be punished with everlasting destruction from the presence of the Lord" (2 Thessalonians 1:9), these "have their part in the lake which burneth with fire and brimstone: which is the second death" (Revelation 21:8).

THE IMMORTAL BECOMES A MORTAL

The words "immortal" and "immortality" when used in Scripture in reference to man find their application to the body. The body of our first parent, as God created him, was an immortal body created to endless existence. God had warned Adam and Eve against eating the fruit of the tree of the knowledge of good and evil, saying: "In the day that thou eatest thereof thou shalt surely die" (Genesis 2:17). In spite of the Lord's warning, they disobeyed, and immediately death began its work in the body. The immortal had put on mortality. Paul says: "Wherefore, as by one man sin entered into the world, and *death by sin*" (Romans 5:12). So then, says the writer to the Hebrews, "It is appointed unto men once to die" (Hebrews 9:27). And again we read in First Corinthians, "In Adam all die" (1 Corinthians 15:22). Over all of the human race, having received its natural life from Adam, hangs the sentence of death. Mortality is the curse upon our race as the result of sin and is the saddest fact in world history. The body of man does not possess immortality by nature, but he is a mortal being—subject to death.

DELIVERANCE FROM MORTALITY

The purpose of the coming of our Lord Jesus Christ was to offer redemption to the fallen race. No mortal could have done this. The dead cannot impart life. The only way that man could escape the sentence of death was by "the appearing of our Lord Jesus Christ. . . . Who only hath immortality" (1 Timothy 6.14, 16).

The soul of man, though retaining endless existence, became morally degenerate. After the fall, his body became corruptible, and his spirit lost all relationship with God. But a glorious truth is given us by the Apostle Paul. He says: "The appearing of our Saviour Jesus Christ, hath abolished death, and hath brought life and immortality to light through the gospel" (2 Timothy 1:10). O wondrous thought! The Immortal One became mortal, "obedient unto death (Philippians 2:8), that He might redeem man's soul, restore his spirit to right relation with God and make his body heir to incorruptibility. This is the triumph of the cross of Christ. By His death and resurrection from the grave our Lord "abolished death". He was willing to be clothed with mortality "that through death He might destroy him that had the power of death, that is, the devil" (Hebrews 2:14). "For as in Adam all die, *even so in Christ shall all be made alive*" (1 Corinthians 15:22).

ETERNAL LIFE AND IMMORTALITY

It seems to the writer that the subject under consideration is made clearer as we see a difference between eternal life and immortality. The terms are not synonymous. The moment one trusts Jesus Christ for salvation he receives everlasting life. This is God's gift bestowed to the sinner upon his acceptance of Jesus Christ as his own personal Saviour from sin. "He that believeth on the Son hath everlasting life" (John 3:36). "He that believeth on Me hath everlasting life" (John 6:47). "But these are written, that ye might believe that Jesus is the Christ, the Son of God; and that believing ye might have life through His Name" (John 20:31). The glorious work of redemption for sinners is effective in any individual just as soon as he is born again, but it cannot be correctly stated that at that moment the soul became immortal. As a matter of fact the soul never lost its immortality. Regeneration by the Holy Spirit is but the beginning of the redemptive process. Immediately upon the Holy Spirit's taking residence in man's spirit, the soul receives eternal life. But the body, even though it has become heir to immortality and incorruptibility, must die. The only possibility the Christian has of his body escaping death and the grave is the return of Christ to rapture all believers to Himself. It follows then that one can possess and enjoy eternal life while death and the grave stare him in the face.

But is this the best that God can offer man? Must our bodies suffer disease, pain, and disability to be put into the ground and to disappear forever? This is where God effects the consummation of the redemptive process. The Apostle Paul says: "We ourselves groan within ourselves, waiting for the adoption, to wit, the redemption of our body" (Romans 8:23). But is there any guarantee that this corruptible body will put on incorruption? Can we be certain that the mortal will one day be clothed with immortality? We only say that in order to fulfill the redemption covenant and promise, Jesus Christ is under oath and obligation to raise the bodies of all the dead who died trusting in Him. There is bright hope and full assurance in the words of our Lord: "I am the resurrection, and the life: he that believeth in Me, though he were dead, yet shall he live" (John 11:25). Our Lord's own testimony assures us of the deliverance from death and decay to life and immortality.

The redemption of the soul is past, but the redemption of the body is still future. Since man is a trinity, and all three component parts of him must be united, it can only be possible as man is restored once again to the image and likeness of God. This is exactly what takes place at the resurrection "when man—the unit— with his tripartite nature is reconstructed into an immortal." The Gospel did not have its consummation with the death of Christ. Paul said: "I declare unto you the Gospel . . . how that Christ died for our sins according to the Scriptures; and that He was buried, and that He rose again the third day according to the Scriptures" (1 Corinthians 15:1-4). Jesus Christ the Immortal One, became mortal by His death. But it was only temporary mortality. By His resurrection from death and the grave to immortality, the Son of God guarantees the same for all that are His. By the first Adam came mortality and death, and by the Last Adam came life and immortality. "Now is Christ risen from the dead, and become the firstfruits of them that slept . . . But every man in his own order: Christ the firstfruits; afterward they that are Christ's at His coming" (1 Corinthians 15:20, 23). As every child of Adam dies, so will every child of God be raised never to die again.

"They that are Christ's" tells us who shall become immortal. "At His coming!" This tells us when we shall become immortal. Immortality is the final step of redemption when our Lord comes again. It is for the redeemed only, for even as "flesh and blood cannot inherit the kingdom of God; neither doth corruption inherit incorruption" (1 Corinthians 15:5).

"The dead shall be raised incorruptible, and we shall be changed" (1 Corinthians 15:22). Though the body of the believer has decayed in the ground, his spirit is still alive and is the pledge of resurrection life. We read: "But if the Spirit of Him that raised up Jesus from the dead dwell in you, He that raised up Christ from the dead shall also quicken your mortal bodies by His Spirit that dwelleth in you" (Romans

8:11). If the Holy Spirit, who is the Spirit of Life, is dwelling in you, by that same Spirit will our mortal bodies be quickened into newness of life. This is the victory that Christ wrought for us by His Death and Resurrection. He took hold of death and, grappling with it, compelled it to let go while He ascended triumphantly to glory. And now, unhindered by death, all who are His are permitted to follow after Him into glory also. Abraham Kuyper has said that the redeemed of the Lord truly die, but without ever for one moment coming under the power of death. Giving up the ghost, breathing out the last breath, is for them nothing but passing through the gate, which from this world leads to the world which is with God; and thus for him who dies in Jesus, it is nothing but a passage into eternal life.

One day the Apostle Paul uttered a self-despairing cry, "O wretched man that I am! Who shall deliver me from the body of this death?" The body, yet unredeemed and under the law of sin and death, is a "body of death." But Paul continues: "I thank God (there is deliverance) through Jesus Christ our Lord" (Romans 7:24, 25). Death may seem to triumph for a season as it enters into our homes, and, one by one, takes those nearest and dearest to us. But death cannot be triumphant over the believer in Christ, "for this corruptible must put on incorruption, and this mortal must put on immortality. So when this corruptible shall have put on incorruption, and this mortal shall have put on immortality, then shall be brought to pass the saying that is written, Death is swallowed up in victory" (1 Corinthians 15:53, 54). The child of God has lost all fear of death, and he can look into a grave unafraid. One day I stood by the grave of my godly grandmother and lifted my heart in praise and gratitude to God that death and the grave were conquered by the risen Saviour. I am looking for the return of Christ and that glad day when the graves shall be opened and the dead in Christ shall rise first, and together we shall sing: "O death, where is thy sting? O grave, where is thy victory?"

> "Thanks be to God, which giveth us the victory through our Lord Jesus Christ" (1 Corinthians 15:55, 57).

"NEW BODIES FOR OLD!"

A well known magazine recently published an article entitled "New Bodies For Old." The purpose of the article was to show the progress that science had made toward giving new arms and legs for lost ones and eyes that can see to men who were blind. Finally, it predicted that an entirely new body may some day be exchanged for an old one, "retaining the developed brain." It concluded by saying, "How many thousands of years in the future all this may be is uncertain." How foolish of the scientific mind to think that it is possible to produce earthly immortality, letting God out of the picture!

The subject of immortality is not of human origin. The Biblical conception of immortality commences with man being in right relation to God, and such relationship he cannot attain by human effort. Man must acknowledge the immortal Christ as his only hope for life after death. Without the Cross of Christ there could have been no redemption for the fallen race, and without that redemption there can be no hope for the life that is immortal. The Christian possesses a living hope that finds its root in the Person and Work of the now living Christ. The Apostle Peter affirms: "Blessed be the God and Father of our Lord Jesus Christ, which according to His abundant mercy hath begotten us again unto a lively (or a living) hope by the resurrection of Jesus Christ from the dead" (1 Peter 1:3). Though eternal life and immortality are not synonymous terms, still there can be no immortality of the body where the spirit of man has not received eternal life through personal faith in the Lord Jesus Christ. Our Lord could say to His disciples: "Because I live, ye shall live also" (John 14:19). The resurrection of believers is guaranteed by Christ's own resurrection.

Edward Rees has said that it is the preaching of immortality which keeps alive the flame of devotion upon the altars of the hearts of men. The Apostle Paul, who, apart from our Lord, was doubtless the greatest preacher of all time, repeatedly held before Christians this glorious truth. His messages were all Christocentric and they directed his hearers heavenward "from whence also we look for the Saviour, the Lord Jesus Christ: Who shall change our vile body, that it may be fashioned like unto His glorious body, according to the working whereby He is able even to subdue all things unto Himself" (Philippians 3:20, 21). This all-glorious fact is the conquering hope of the Church. William Jennings Bryan has given us a beautiful paragraph on the subject—

> If the Father deigns to touch with divine power the cold and pulseless heart of the buried acorn, and make it burst forth from its prison walls, will He leave neglected in the earth the man, who was made in the image of his Creator? If He stoops to give to the rosebush, whose leaves and withered blossoms float upon the breeze, the sweet assurance of another springtime, will He withhold the words of hope from the souls of men when the frosts of death's winter come? If matter, mute and inanimate, though changed by the forces of nature into a

multitude of forms, can never die, will the imperial spirit of man suffer annihilation after it has paid a brief visit, like a royal guest, to this tenement of clay? Rather let us believe that He who in His apparent prodigality wastes not the raindrop, the blade of grass or the evening's zephyr, but makes them all carry out His eternal plans, has given immortality to the mortal, and gathered to Himself the generous spirit of our friends."

In the hour of death and separation from our loved ones we have this comforting belief that the grave is but the gateway to glory. May God grant that you, dear reader, shall receive eternal life and a victorious faith in a life after death.

CHAPTER FOUR

THE CONSCIOUSNESS OF THE SOUL AFTER DEATH

I S the soul conscious after death? This is not a new question. For centuries there have been certain religionists who have contended that the soul *existed* after death but that it was *not conscious*. Upon investigation, some of you may be surprised to know of the wide-spread belief in the teaching of the sleeping of the soul. Because of the universal interest in the whereabouts of the dead, false sects prey upon the public, claiming complete knowledge of the subject. Such groups as "Jehovah's Witnesses," spiritualists and others have spread the sophistical conclusion that at death the body returns to dust and the soul becomes unconscious.

Such statements as the following are but a few of the distortions and perversions of the Holy Scriptures that have to do with the soul after death. "At death, it is not the body but the soul which dies." "The interim from death until the soul is resurrected is one of unconsciousness." "Even the apostles were unconscious for centuries." These assertions are being made by the advocates of the teachings of Russell and Rutherford, but they are the views of the men themselves, imposed upon the Holy Scriptures. These ideas were read into the Bible, but were never in the mind of the inspired writers.

MAN IS CREATED TO ENDLESS EXISTENCE

Every human being enters the world possessed with *endless existence*. It is true that at death the soul is separated from the body. It is not consistent with the teaching of the Bible to say that at death the soul lapses into a state of complete unconsciousness or even into a deep sleep. If at first glance it would seem that the Bible teaches this, then we will do well to examine those passages where death is referred to as sleep. The few texts that mendacious scholars have dislodged from their context in order to prove that physical death is the cessation of all consciousness can be easily and understandingly explained when interpreted in the light of the many other passages that deal with this subject.

In Ecclesiastes we read: "The dead know not anything" (Ecclesiastes 9:5). Certainly we all agree that a dead and deteriorating body has absolutely no consciousness of anything past, present, or future. But are the advocates of "soul-sleep" justified in using the above text as evidence of the unconscious state of the soul after death? We believe that this method of using a text to support a false theory that elsewhere is denied in Scripture, proves that those who stoop to such methods either are untruthful or deficient. Those who teach "soul-sleep" will find it quite difficult to harmonize their views with other statements that are made by the same writer of Ecclesiastes—

> "Then shall the dust return to the earth as it was: and the spirit shall return unto God Who gave it" (Ecclesiastes 12:7).

> "All go unto one place; for all are of the dust, and all turn to dust again" (Ecclesiastes 3:20).

Now we know that this verse is speaking of the body, for in the next verse we read :

> "Who knoweth the spirit of man that goeth upward?" (Ecclesiastes 3:21).

ONLY MAN'S BODY DIES (OR SLEEPS)

In Scripture we read that man sleeps, but the sleep always is identified with the body. Never once does the Bible refer to the soul sleeping. Where some fall into danger is in identifying man merely with his body and in ignoring the fact that he is a triune being. Man is a trinity; body, soul and spirit. Now the body is not the whole man. Therefore it cannot be concluded that the death of the body is the death of the whole man.

Another misconstrued verse is found in the prophecy of Daniel where we read:

> "And many of them that sleep in the dust of the earth shall awake, some to everlasting life, and some to shame and everlasting contempt" (Daniel 12:2).

Some scholars question whether this verse has anything to do with physical resurrection. Dr. A. C. Gaebelein in his commentary on Daniel says that, if physical resurrection were taught in this verse, the passage would clash with the revelation concerning resurrection in the New Testament, for there is no general resurrection for the righteous and wicked together. "We repeat the passage has nothing to do with physical resurrection. Physical resurrection is however used as a figure of the national revival of Israel in that day. They have been sleeping nationally in the dust of the earth, buried among the Gentiles. But at that time there will take place a national restoration, a bringing together of the house of Judah and of Israel. It is the same figure as used in the vision of the dry bones in Ezekiel 37. This vision is employed by the men, who have invented the theory of a second chance and larger hope for the wicked dead to back up their evil teaching; but anyone can see that it is not a bodily resurrection, but a national revival and restoration of that people. Their national graves, not literal burying places, will be opened and the Lord will bring them forth out of all the countries into which they have been scattered. The same distinction holds good which we have already pointed out. The great mass of Jews, who cast their belief in God and His Word to the winds, who accepted the man of sin and acknowledged the wicked King, will face everlasting contempt, but the remnant will possess all things promised to them and become the heirs of that Kingdom, which is prepared from the foundation of the world. And besides the national blessing which they receive, they will be in possession of everlasting life, for they are born again." We have given this rather lengthy quotation for the reason that some readers may not be acquainted with this view.

However, even if the above interpretation of verse two is not correct, but a physical resurrection is intended, certainly Daniel would not be referring to anything except the resurrection of the body. We are not to conclude for one moment that the word "sleep" applies to any other part of man except his body.

THE NEW TESTAMENT TEACHES MAN'S ENDLESS CONSCIOUS EXISTENCE

The citation of a few New Testament verses make it clear that man's conscious existence is endless.

> "And the graves were opened; and many *bodies* of the saints which slept arose" (Matthew 27:52).

Please notice how the Holy Spirit says that the "bodies" slept. Jesus said:

> "Our friend Lazarus *sleepeth;* but I go, that I may awake him out of sleep . . . Then said Jesus unto them plainly, Lazarus is *dead*" (John 11:11, 14).

Death to our Lord was never anything more than sleep. It is a figure of speech that the Bible applies, for there is never a pause in our consciousness. It was the body of Lazarus that was dead. It was his body that Martha said "stinketh: for he hath been dead four days." When Jesus said plainly that Lazarus was *dead,* He could mean only his body, for when He added: "I go, that I may awake Him out of sleep," He did this by raising the *body* of Lazarus from death and the grave. We read in verse forty-four: *"And he that was dead came forth, bound hand and foot with grave clothes."* The part of Lazarus that was dead was that part of him that was bound "hand and foot, and his face."

Since the soul of man never dies, and the soul is as much a part of man as is his body, then we may say that the dead are alive. The writer became convinced that there was never a pause in man's consciousness while thinking upon the last words of dying men. Think for a moment of our Lord's last words as He hung dying upon the Cross. He said: "Father, into Thy hands I commend my spirit: and having said thus, He gave up the ghost" (Luke 23:46). Only a little over three decades before, Christ had come from the presence of the Father, His spirit having taken its abode in the body prepared by God in the womb of the Virgin. He came to bring life and immortality to light through His Gospel. He came, not to bring immortality, but to reveal it and to show man that he could have everlasting life.

By finishing His task He fulfilled every demand of God's righteous law. He offered His life a ransom for sin, and then departed this life. Jesus knew that His Father was watching, listening eagerly and intently; so with every confidence, He spoke to the Father with the consciousness that His task was well done. Then His words, "Into Thy hands I commend My

Spirit," is the doctrine of immortality. Here Christ is teaching the world the survival of the spiritual part of man after his physical body has died. Death to Jesus was but a passage into the presence of God, not a cold unconscious condition. He knew all about life after death, and He left us with divine assurance that only the body dies. The spirit continues to exist in a conscious state.

Another of our Lord's last words from the Cross proves that death touches only the physical part of man. Let us give consideration to the malefactor hanging on the cross next to the Lord Jesus. This man had not joined the jeering mob, but instead he acknowledged Christ in the face of the Roman opposition. With a contrite spirit and simple faith he said: "Jesus, Lord, remember me when Thou comest into Thy kingdom" (Luke 23:42). The world shall never forget the words which Jesus answered the dying thief. With the soul of this criminal at the very portals of Hell, the dying Saviour said to the dying sinner: "Today shalt thou be with me in Paradise." They were killing his body to be sure, but Jesus promised him that there would be no time of waiting, no pause of sleep or unconsciousness of the soul. Jesus assured him that before that very day had come to a close, he would still be alive and with Christ in Paradise. These words of Christ from the Cross manifest the supreme confidence that He had in a place of blissful life immediately after the believer takes his departure from this earth. If we are called away from this earth today, then "today"—not at some distant period—but immediately, on that very day we shall ascend into His presence. The death of the body is the gateway into a fuller and larger life into which the soul passes.

There will be no sluggishness nor insensibility after death. Dr. Rimmer writes: "The phenomenon of sleep is peculiar to the flesh alone. The soul, the spirit, and the mentality never sleep, and that is why we dream. In that great study that is called the psychology of dreams, it is conceded that all dreams are the result of past experience. The past experiences may be either mental or physical, but all dreams are predicated upon some past event. When the body succumbs to the influence of sleep, the spirit or soul, in which is resident the consciousness of self, goes off on the amazing peregrinations that men call dreams." There is a remarkable power of the subconscious mind even when the body is asleep.

The martyrdom of Stephen is a strong argument in favor of the supremacy and the survival of the spiritual part of man. When they stoned Stephen to death, we read that "he fell asleep." This could have no reference whatever to the soul, for it was his body they had pummeled with rocks. As Stephen's body went to its death, earth was receding but Heaven's gate approaching. He knew that he was entering into another sphere of the living. He prayed: "Lord Jesus, receive my spirit" (Acts 7:59). This disciple of Christ did not seek to postpone death or to fight it off. His murderers held no fear for him. He remembered the words of Jesus: "Be not afraid of them that kill the body, and after that have no more that they can do" (Luke 12:4). It is the assurance of immortality and eternal life that enables the servants of Jesus Christ to bear suffering, face all opposition, and die if they are called upon to do so. The scoffing and the scorning of the enemies of Christ can never cheat us out of the presence of our Lord and the place that He has prepared for us.

The Apostle Paul gives us a glimpse into his inner life in an experience that appears only once in all of his writings.

"It is not expedient for me doubtless to glory.
I will come to visions and revelations of the
Lord. I knew a man in Christ above fourteen
years ago, (whether in the body, I cannot tell;
or whether out of the body, I cannot tell: God
knoweth;) such an one caught up to the third
heaven. And I knew such a man, (whether in
the body, or out of the body, I cannot tell; God
knoweth;) How that he was caught up into paradise, and heard unspeakable words, which it is
not lawful for a man to utter" (2 Corinthians
12:1-4)

In this singular but rich experience of Paul's there
is valuable material that bears upon our subject. So
personal and sacred was this experience that Paul is
reticent to tell. There is no doubt that the mighty
Apostle is referring to himself although he refers to
himself in the third person. Fourteen years before the
writing of this Epistle, Paul says that he was caught
up into the "third heaven," also called "paradise." The
Bible speaks of three heavens. There is the atmospheric heaven in which the birds fly, the heaven where
the stars shine, and the third heaven, called paradise,
where God is and where His glory is set forth. It was
into the third heaven, into the presence of God, where
the great apostle was taken. If we study the chronology
of Paul's journeys and labors we find that a little more
than fourteen years before he wrote his Epistle to the
Corinthians he was laboring at Lystra (Acts 14:19).
There the Jews stoned him and dragged him outside
the city supposing he had been dead. It is generally
believed that his experience in paradise to which he
refers took place at Lystra while he lay unconscious.
He tells us that he was so enraptured by the glories
that he saw in Heaven that he did not know whether
or not he was there in body—"whether in the body, I
cannot tell; or whether out of the body, I cannot tell:

God knoweth." Do not overlook the teaching here. It is possible to be fully conscious and yet be absent from the body. Such clear and unmistakable teaching as this of the Apostle Paul defies and defeats the theory of "soul-sleep."

There are three accounts of our Lord's raising the dead. Each time He approached the dead and spoke to him as if he were alive. To the son of the widow of Nain He said: "Young man, I say unto thee, Arise" (Luke 7:14). When Christ came to the daughter of Jairus, we are told: "He took her by the hand, and called, saying, Maid, arise" (Luke 8:54). Finally, He said to the brother of Mary and Martha: "Lazarus, come forth" (John 11:43). In each case Jesus speaks to the person as if he were alive. We can only answer that each was alive. As G. Campbell Morgan says: "The body was dead. The man was not dead. No man is ever dead when his body lies dead!" The soul of man will never enter into a state of non-existence nor unconsciousness.

In Christ's account of the rich man and Lazarus we have the matter summed up and settled that the soul is conscious after death. Both men died and were buried. Though their bodies were in the graves, each of them was alive and conscious. The rich man in Hell could see, hear, speak, and feel (Luke 16:19-31).

Let the unsaved heed God's warning. There is a life after death. The unsaved and the saved will be separated from each other. The lost will doubtless carry with them some memories of the past, and their retribution for rejecting Christ will be endless.

But let the believer take courage and be comforted. When we move out of this tabernacle, the real man will leave the body and enter into the presence of the Lord.

CHAPTER FIVE

THE TWO RESURRECTIONS

THE resurrection of the human body from the grave is clearly taught in God's Word. Job, the oldest of the patriarchs, said: "For I know that my Redeemer liveth, and that He shall stand at the latter day upon the earth: And though after my skin worms destroy this body, yet in my flesh shall I see God" (Job 19:25, 26). It is evident that Job was firm in his belief in the resurrection of his body and a future life beyond the grave.

Abraham, the founder and father of his race, lived to be one hundred seventy-five years old, and "died in a good old age" (Genesis 25:7, 8), but "he looked for a city which hath foundations, whose builder and maker is God" (Hebrews 11:10). He never saw that city in his earthly pilgrimage, for earth to him was a "strange country." The godly old patriarch shared with others who "desire a better country, that is, an heavenly: wherefore God is not ashamed to be called their God: for He hath prepared for them a city" (Hebrews 11:16). But Abraham believed that the heavenly city would be inhabited by a fleshly body, "accounting that God was able to raise him up, even from the dead . . ." (Hebrews 11:19).

David was confident of a future life. He said: "My flesh also shall rest in hope" (Psalm 16:9), and "I shall be satisfied, when I awake, with Thy likeness" (Psalm 17:15). These words of the man of God refute the erroneous teaching that the resurrection refers to the spirit of man, and not to his body. Neither the soul nor the spirit of man dies, but it is his body which dies and is buried. Therefore it must be the body that is raised from the dead, and not the soul or spirit.

47

When our Lord Jesus was here upon earth, He taught that all men who die will be raised again at some future date. "Marvel not at this: for the hour is coming, in the which *all* that are in the graves shall hear His voice, And shall come forth . . ." (John 5:28, 29). We affirm and avow our belief in the resurrection of the human body from death and the grave. Without this hope our Christian faith is vain, our brightest hopes are merely bursting bubbles, the Bible is not a true and reliable record, the men who wrote it were poor deluded victims of falsehood, and Jesus Christ is the world's biggest impostor. But so clear is the Bible on the subject of the resurrection that we admit no confusion or doubt.

A Wrong Conception

Many people, among them some Christians, have been taught to believe that there is only one "general" resurrection of all the dead at the end of the world. This is a serious error which has robbed many believers of joy and victory in this life. Nowhere in the Scriptures are we taught that the bodies of all men will be raised at the same time. It is true that all the dead will be raised and brought into judgment, but neither the time, the place, nor the judgments are the same. The Bible clearly distinguishes between a first and a second resurrection.

> ". . . All that are in the graves shall hear His voice, and shall come forth; they that have done good, unto the resurrection of life; and they that have done evil, unto the resurrection of damnation" (John 5:28, 29).

When men are raised, not all will be raised at the same time nor in the same condition. There will be two resurrections for two classes of men. One will be raised to eternal life and immortality, while the other will be raised to condemnation and banishment from the presence of the Lord. There is a "resurrection of life" and a "resurrection of damnation."

> "And thou shalt be blessed; for they cannot recompense thee: for thou shalt be recompensed at *the resurrection of the just*" (Luke 14:14).

There is, then, a "resurrecton of the just," and since "all shall come forth," there must of necessity be a resurrection of the unjust. Since the dead in Christ shall rise *first,* the implication is that the dead out of Christ (or without Christ) will be raised *afterwards.* Luke makes no mention in the above passage about a resurrection of the unsaved. Indeed the unsaved shall be raised, but not for a considerable length of time after the saved have been raised. When Paul testified before Felix, he said, "that there shall be a resurrection of the dead, both of the just and unjust" (Acts 24:15). The Apostle John makes a clear distinction between the two. He speaks of the redeemed who "lived and reigned with Christ a thousand years. But the rest of the dead lived not again until the thousand years were finished. This is the first resurrection" (Revelation 20:4, 5).

Every believer has passed out of death into life (John 5:24). His life "is hid with Christ in God" (Colossians 3:3), and the exceeding greatness of God's power in resurrection toward us who believe is the same "mighty power which He wrought in Christ, when He raised Him from the dead" (Ephesians 1:19, 20). And by that same power will all the unbelieving dead be brought out of their graves to stand before the judgment of the Great White Throne.

The First Resurrection

"For the Lord Himself shall descend from heaven
with a shout, and the voice of the archangel, and with
the trump of God; and *the dead in Christ shall rise
first*" (1 Thessalonians 4:16).

Surely language could be no clearer than this—"The
dead in Christ shall rise first." We see first that the time
of the First Resurrection is the coming again of our
Lord Jesus Christ in the clouds of Heaven to rapture
all of the saints to Himself. Here we must distinguish
between Christ's coming for His own before the millennium and His coming again to raise the rest of the
dead (unbelievers) who remained in their graves during the thousand years. Let there be no misunderstand-
ing that it is a settled fact that there is *at least* a one
thousand year interval between the First and the
Second Resurrection. The Apostle John, by Divine inspiration, confirms this—

> "And I saw thrones, and they sat upon them,
> and judgment was given unto them: and I saw
> the souls of them that were beheaded for the
> witness of Jesus, and for the word of God, and
> which had not worshipped the beast, neither
> his image, neither had received his mark upon
> their foreheads, or in their hands; and they lived
> and reigned with Christ a thousand years. But
> the rest of the dead lived not again until the
> thousand years were finished. This is the first
> resurrection" (Revelation 20:4, 5).

At the consummation of the First Resurrection there
are three companies of believers who will have been
raised at different times. Let us say, for clarity, there are
three stages of the resurrection of believers—

> (1) When our Lord was crucified on the
> Cross, we read: "And, behold the veil of the
> temple was rent in twain from the top to the

bottom; and the earth did quake, and the rocks rent;

"And the graves were opened; and many bodies of the saints which slept arose" (Matthew 27:51, 52).

(2) There is the second stage of the First Resurrection to which we already have made mention (1 Thessalonians 4:16), when all true believers are raised at the first appearance of Christ. To this we add the Apostle Paul's word in First Corinthians—"In a moment, in the twinkling of an eye, at the last trump: for the trumpet shall sound, and the dead shall be raised incorruptible, and we shall be changed" (1 Corinthians 15:52).

(3) The third and final stage of the First Resurrection occurs about seven years after the resurrection of saints at Christ's coming at the rapture. "Those resurrected near the close of the seven years' period of tribulation are the multitude of believers who were led to the truth through the witness of the 144,000." Because they would not receive the mark of the beast in their hands and foreheads, they were martyred. These are brought forth from the dead at the end of the Tribulation just before Christ comes to earth to reign for one thousand years.

CHRIST THE FIRSTFRUITS

"But now is Christ risen from the dead, and become the firstfruits of them that slept. For since by man came death, by man came also the resurrection of the dead. For as in Adam all die, even so in Christ shall all be made alive. But every man in his own order: Christ the firstfruits; afterward they that are Christ's at his coming" (1 Corinthians 15:20-23).

The word "Firstfruits" is a significant one. In the ceremony of the Israelites there were certain national feasts kept annually. The third in order of these was the *Feast of Firstfruits,* an annual occasion of consecration that was solemnized at the beginning of harvest time.

> "And the Lord spake unto Moses, saying, Speak unto the children of Israel, and say unto them, When ye be come into the land which I give unto you, and shall reap the harvest thereof, then ye shall bring a sheaf of the firstfruits of your harvest unto the priest" (Leviticus 23:9, 10).

Dr. Martin DeHaan points out that the harvest was divided into three parts. It was one harvest, the fruit of one season, presented on three different occasions. First, there was the sheaf of firstfruits, the earnest or pledge of the greater harvest that would follow. This beautifully typifies the Resurrection of Christ who, by coming forth from the tomb, accomplished the work of the redemption and guaranteed for all who believe in Him a greater resurrection when He returns. "But now is Christ risen from the dead, and become the *firstfruits* of them that slept" (1 Corinthians 15:20). Just as the firstfruits were a pledge of the coming harvest that would be presented to Jehovah, so our Lord's Resurrection is a promise that all who are in their graves who have died trusting Him will be raised and brought into the presence of the Father. Speaking to believers, the Apostle Paul, by the Holy Spirit, says: "For as in Adam all die, even so in Christ shall all be made alive."

After the firstfruits followed the harvesting of the larger part of the crops. We read: "Christ the firstfruits; afterward they that are Christ's at His coming" (1 Corinthians 15:23). Our risen Lord is now in Heaven. Even so, "Our conversation is in Heaven; from whence also we look for the Saviour, the Lord

Jesus Christ: who shall change our vile body, that it may be fashioned like unto His glorious body, according to the working whereby He is able even to subdue all things unto Himself" (Philippians 3:20, 21). Our physical bodies have in them sickness, weakness and death, but our all-powerful, all-victorious Saviour has said: "I am He that liveth, and was dead; and, behold, I am alive for evermore, Amen; and have the keys of hell and of death" (Revelation 1:18). He will come again even as He said. Christ the firstfruits; afterward they that are Christ's at His coming.

But the harvest is not ended as yet. It is not completed until the gleanings are added. Always there are loose ears that fall by the way, and these must be gathered up. This is called the gleaning. We recall how Ruth "came, and gleaned in the field after the reapers" (Ruth 2:3). The gleanings are those tribulation saints who had not heard and believed the Gospel before the rapture of the Church. So we have Christ the firstfruits, then we have the harvest or the resurrection of the saved at the rapture, and finally the gleanings or the saved of the seven years' tribulation period. Then follows the millennial age during which all the saints of every age will reign with Christ a thousand years. What bright prospect for those who put their trust in the Son of God! But tell me, are you prepared for the coming of the Lord and the First Resurrection?

THE SECOND RESURRECTION

When the thousand years are expired, Satan will be loosed for a season and will carry on his rebellion where he left off before the millennium when he was cast into the bottomless pit. Then God will have done with Satan forever, for "the devil that deceived them was cast into the lake of fire and brimstone, where the beast and the false prophet are, and shall be tormented day and night for ever and ever" (Revelation 20:10). We shudder at this unceasing torment without intermission, this never-ending existence in painful agony.

But the devil's doom is not the blackest page in the Biblical records of God's dealings. There is yet an account to be settled with all those who died in rejection of the Lord Jesus Christ. A Great White Throne has been erected. We are about to view the greatest assize ever conducted. The Judge is our Lord Jesus Himself, for "The Father judgeth no man, but hath committed all judgment unto the Son" (John 5:22). Here the hated and despised Nazarene will sit in righteous judgment of all who refused to acknowledge His Messiahship and Saviourhood. It is the gloomiest hour for that part of the human race that spurned the love of God and denied His only begotten Son. This is the resurrection of the unbelieving dead. There are those who remained "dead in trespasses and sins" (Ephesians 2:1). Though they are spiritually dead having not eternal life, they are standing before God physically alive in their resurrection bodies. From every part of the earth the bodies of the wicked dead are raised to receive the final sentence, banishment from the presence of God and eternal punishment in the lake of fire.

The final resurrection occurs. John says: "I saw the dead, small and great, stand before God; . . . The sea gave up the dead which were in it; and death and hell delivered up the dead which were in them: and they were judged every man according to their works" (Revelation 20:12, 14). Who will be judged here? The answer is that there will not be one single believer in Christ that will appear before the judgment of the Great White Throne. Only the unsaved will be there, appearing in a physical body to be condemned to

Hell. All will be there by their own personal choice. "As I live, saith the Lord God, I have no pleasure in the death of the wicked" (Ezekiel 33:11). "The Lord is not willing that any should perish, but that all should come to repentance" (2 Peter 3:9). You had your opportunity to accept Jesus Christ as personal Saviour, but you turned from Him, and by so doing you have chosen eternal torment in the lake of fire. "For God sent not His Son into the world to condemn the world; but that the world through Him might be saved. He that believeth on Him is not condemned; but he that believeth not is condemned already, because he hath not believed in the name of the only begotten Son of God" (John 3:17, 18).

Many unbelievers seek to stifle their conscience by uttering their unbelief in a physical resurrection. They count it a thing incredible that God could raise a physical body that had been trampled under the dust for more than one thousand years. Certainly God knows where the dust is, and since He fashioned the body of Adam out of particles of dust, it is only reasonable to believe that He can fashion it again. The world is His, and the fullness thereof. He fixed the stars in their courses and named them all; the wind and the waves obey His will; the innumerable grains of sand by the seashores are under His divine control; He numbers every hair on our heads. The logical reasoning of any thinking mind and the inner convictions of the honest man tell us plainly how foolish one is to deny the existence of life after death.

The Resurrection of Jesus Christ is the confirmation of the resurrection of the human body and future judgment. When the mighty Apostle Paul preached his sermon to the Athenians on Mars' hill, he said that God commands all men everywhere to repent, "because He hath appointed a day, in the which He will judge the world in righteousness by that Man whom He hath ordained; whereof He hath given assurance unto all men, in that He hath raised Him from the dead" (Acts 17:31). It is true that man died here, but since both his Judge and his day of judgment already have been appointed, he must be raised after death if the purposes of God are to be fulfilled. Certainly they are not dead men whom God will arraign before his solemn tribunal. They will be alive and conscious of that great hour. So in order that man might be assured of a future judgment, Christ arose as the criterion of the law of resurrection. The living Christ is a positive attestation of the fact that there is a day of judgment. We are not intimating nor are we presuming a day of judgment, but we are merely standing with the Apostle Paul in affirming a positive assurance God gave to the world when He raised Jesus Christ from the dead. We read in "The Apostles' Creed" how Christ ". . . was crucified, dead and buried; the third day He arose again from the dead; He ascended into heaven, and sitteth on the right hand of God the Father Almighty; from thence He shall come to judge the quick and the dead . . ."

The last judgment in the Bible will be that of the unsaved dead who will stand before the Great White Throne in living, resurrected bodies to receive their final sentence of doom and be cast into the lake of fire. This will not be a judgment to see if sinners are lost, for they are lost already because "he that believeth not is condemned already" (John 3:18). Christians will be present, but only as witnesses. The judged will be those of the Second Resurrection whose bodies have been brought out of the grave and whose spirits brought back from Hell.

All of the unsaved, "small and great, stand before God" (Revelation 20:12). In our human courts of law it is often the case that the defendant does not appear. Sometimes a witness, a juror, or a judge can be bribed, and the guilty one escapes trial and the passing of sentence. Sometimes false witnesses can turn court's evidence and the guilty one goes free. But in that day, the books are opened, including the Book of Life, "and the dead were judged out of those things which were written in the books according to their works" (Revelation 20:12). While it is true that millions have lived and died of whom the world knows nothing, their thoughts and deeds are divinely written where the memory of them can never perish. An accurately guided hand has recorded the biography of all, and all evil will be accounted for in that dreadfully solemn hour. If you have despised Jesus here, it will mean judgment there. If you have belittled the invitation to Heaven while here, you will be cast into Hell then.

A LITERAL, PHYSICAL BODY

God has said by the prophet Isaiah: "Unto Me every knee shall bow, every tongue shall swear" (Isaiah 45:23). The Apostle Paul quoting Isaiah, said: "For it is written, As I live, saith the Lord, every knee shall bow to me, and every tongue shall confess to God" (Romans 14:11). Then the Apostle adds: "Wherefore God also hath highly exalted Him (Jesus), and given Him a name which is above every name: That at the Name of Jesus every knee should bow . . . and that every tongue should confess that Jesus Christ is Lord, to the glory of God the Father" (Philippians 2:9-11). Only a part of the human race has agreed with the testimony of God the Father which He has given concerning His Son. But at the final judgment, every unbeliever of every age will bow the knee that once he refused to bend, and confess with the tongue that once he refused to confess Christ with. Yes, literal knees and tongues of every Christ-rejecting sinner will bow and confess in utter humility the Christ they spurned and scoffed at here on earth.

Again we repeat that God finds no pleasure in the death of the wicked. He would rather save than have them die in unbelief, but whosoever is not found written in the Book of Life will be cast into the lake of fire. They shall have their part in the lake which burns with fire and brimstone. This is the second death (Revelation 20:15; 21:8). If you die in your sins, the judgment is sure and certain. You will not escape! No, you cannot escape. If, while you read this message, you realize your need of Christ as your personal Saviour from sin, confess that you are a sinner and trust Christ to save you. "Blessed and holy is he that hath part in the first resurrection" (Revelation 20:6).

CHAPTER SIX

THE RESURRECTION BODY

"With what body do they come?" (1 Corinthians 15:35).

DEATH—THE SLEEP OF THE BODY

NO Biblical description of death is so comforting and consoling to the believer as that which is revealed in the familiar word *sleep*. It is a word that applies to the body only and never to the soul. Our Lord said to His disciples: "Our friend Lazarus *sleepeth;* but I go that I may awake him out of sleep. Then said His disciples, Lord, if he sleep, he shall do well. Howbeit Jesus spake of his death" (John 11:11-13). Of the martyrdom and death of Stephen, we read: "He fell *asleep*" (Acts 7:60). When the Apostle Paul was yet alive, he said that of the five hundred brethren who had seen Christ alive after His Resurrection, "some are fallen *asleep*" (1 Corinthians 15:6). His comforting message to the believers at Thessalonica was, "I would not have you to be ignorant, brethren, concerning them which are *asleep*" (1 Thessalonians 4:13). The Apostle Peter, speaking of Old Testament saints, said: "The fathers fell *asleep*" (2 Peter 3:4).

The Old Testament saints were comforted by this same truth. More than forty times in the Old Testament it is said of a man who died that he "slept with his fathers." "And the LORD said unto Moses, Behold, thou shalt sleep with thy fathers" (Deuteronomy 31:16; 2 Samuel 7:12). Job said: "Now shall I sleep in the dust; and thou shalt seek me in the morning, but I shall not be" (Job 7:21). In these verses we have a transcendently sublime description of death which assures the believer that it is but "the transient slumber of the body, to be followed by the glorious awakening at the sound of the last trumpet."[1]

DEATH—A TEMPORARY SEPARATION OF THE SPIRITUAL FROM THE PHYSICAL

This temporary suspension of the activities of the body does not mean that the spirit of man is asleep. The body is but the tabernacle or dwelling place of the spirit part of man. Upon the death of the body, the spirit of a believer takes departure, closing the senses of the body until the day of its resurrection. Immediately upon the death of our bodies, we leave the flesh, "to depart, and to be with Christ" (Philippians 1:23), "waiting for the adoption, to wit, the redemption of our body" (Romans 8:23).

Here is a simple illustration. Recently I noticed that a butcher shop in our town was no longer open for business. One day while driving past the building I saw a sign in the window which read: "Closed For Alterations". The owner had suspended his business relations with the public long enough to renovate the store. After about two months the store was reopened with many changes. This is a picture of the death of the believer. He moves out of the body until it has been repaired and renovated, when, at the resurrection, the inward man shall move into his renewed body.[2]

RAISED TO BE LIKE JESUS

Death is not to be feared by the Christian. We shall live in a literal body just as real as the one we have now, for, says Paul: "We look for the Saviour, the Lord Jesus Christ: Who shall change our vile body, that it may be fashioned like unto His glorious body. . . ."

[1] T. L. Cuyler
[2] The use of this illustration was suggested by Dr. H. A. Ironside in "Death and Afterwards".

(Philippians 3:20, 21). The coming of our Lord in the air to take us to Heaven will necessitate a change in this purchased body of corruption. The body is as much the Lord's purchased possession as is the soul. It is dear to Him. "The body is . . . for the Lord; and the Lord for the body" (1 Corinthians 6:13). The goal of the Gospel is to bring eternal life and immortality to all who will believe. Since the body of the saints will be "fashioned like unto His glorious body", we may well wonder what our bodies will be like at the resurrection. John says: "We know that, when He shall appear, we shall be like Him; for we shall see Him as He is" (1 John 3:2). When our Lord ascended into Heaven, He was thirty-three years of age, a young man in the strength and glory of His youth. Senility had not overtaken our Lord when He died upon the Cross for our sins. In David's Psalm of the exalted Christ in the glory, we read: "Thou hast the dew of Thy youth" (Psalm 110:3). O wondrous thought! We shall be clothed upon with perennial youth. We shall be like Him, fashioned like unto His glorious body.

Christ shall "*change* our vile body" (Philippians 3:21) we read. The word "change" means to *transfigure*. It has been suggested that we have here the thought of metamorphosis which is a remarkable change in the form and structure of a living body. When our Lord took Peter, James, and John up into the Holy Mountain, we read that "He was *transfigured* before them" (Matthew 17:2). Christ appeared during that brief period of time in His glorified body. He was transfigured (or metamorphosed) before them. It was a body like His post-resurrection body when He appeared to His disciples behind shut doors (John 20:19). The change of the believer at the resurrection has to do with his body, wherein resides the sin principle, for even the Christian must admit, "I know that in me (that is in my flesh), there dwelleth no good thing" (Romans 7:18). The word "change" could not refer to the spiritual part of man, for, as Kenneth Wuest says: "The word 'change' is the translation of a Greek word which speaks of an expression which is assumed from the outside, which act brings about a change of outward expression".[1]

Biologically speaking, the change of a caterpillar into a butterfly is spoken of as a "metamorphosis". The ugly, repulsive caterpillar is confined to a tomb which it spins for itself. While in the cocoon there is an apparently dead and formless substance. But after the warm sun of spring has beaten its golden rays upon that cocoon, there comes forth a beautiful butterfly. Though the butterfly is different in appearance from the caterpillar, we recognize the beautiful winged insect as being the same as the caterpillar. It is the same living creature, yet different. So also is the resurrection of the body. Now we have a vile body (or a body of humiliation). The Apostle James calls it a "low" body, "because as the flower of the grass he shall pass away" (James 1:10). The body of Adam, in its original state, was provided with a covering of glory, but when sin entered, the covering of glory was replaced with a covering of humiliation. In our present bodies of humiliation we are unfit for the glories of Heaven and God's presence, but hopefully we look for our Lord's return when He shall fashion our bodies of humiliation like unto His own body of glory. It will be the same body in that it will be recognizable, but wonderfully changed.

Answering The Skeptic

Some unbelieving skeptics have proposed the argument that it will be impossible for the same body to

[1] "Philippians in the Greek New Testament".

be raised since the bodies of those who have been dead for hundreds of years have become decomposed into integrant parts; that is, reduced to powder. They add that those elements which composed one body may have become a part of other bodies. For example, a dead body deteriorates. Over the grave of that body a tree may grow, having fed its roots on the elements of the dead body. If the fruit of that tree is eaten by other men, the elements of the decomposed and deteriorated body in the grave become a part of other men's bodies. They conclude that it is an impossibility to raise the same body atom for atom.

God anticipated this problem. We read: "But some man will say, How are the dead raised up? and with what body do they come" (1 Corinthians 15:35)? To answer this, the Apostle, by the Holy Spirit, uses the illustration of a farmer sowing grain. When a farmer drops a kernel of grain into the ground, he knows that when the seed dies or seemingly rots away, that does not mean the end of his efforts. He knows that the one seed will come forth into a fuller life, producing a stalk with several ears bearing many hundreds of kernels like the one he planted. The actual seed that was planted he does not see. Yet there is absolute identity. It is the same with the resurrection of our bodies. "That which thou sowest is not quickened, except it die: And that which thou sowest, thou sowest not that body that shall be, but bare grain, it may chance of wheat, or of some other grain: But God giveth it a body as it hath pleased Him, and to every seed his own body" (1 Corinthians 15:35-38).

It will not be necessary for God to use every part of this body when he raises it from the grave. Such a thought is not taught in Scripture. In fact, it is scientifically true that the component parts of our bodies undergo periodical changes. We are told that through the change of elements, we receive new bodies every seven years. We may not be conscious of the change. Nevertheless we have not the same body today that we had seven years ago. There is an identity that we maintain all of our lifetime, and yet there is not one cell in our bodies that was there seven years ago. In the resurrection the bodies of the saints will bear their individual identities. Dr. Wilbur M. Smith has said: "The fact that after death our physical substance disintegrates and scatters, creates no difficulties for God, so that He could not bring those bodies back gloriously transformed." By the new birth we are born again into the Kingdom of God, a Kingdom that can never break down or disintegrate. Because sin can never enter, there is no danger of corruptibility. The resurrection will be the occasion when our bodies become incorruptible and will inherit the Kingdom of God.[4]

From Corruption to Incorruption
From Mortality to Immortality

"It is sown in corruption; it is raised in incorruption" (1 Corinthians 15:42).

"For this corruptible must put on incorruption" (1 Corinthians 15:53).

Death is written on the face of all that is alive. The moment we begin to live we commence to die. The report of the birth of a new baby guarantees the digging of a new grave. The preacher of wisdom wrote: "The strong men shall bow themselves, and the grinders cease because they are few, and those that look out of the windows be darkened . . . man goeth to his long home, and the mourners go about the streets. . . . Then shall the dust return to the earth as it was: and the spirit shall return unto God who

[4] R. C. H. Lenski

gave it" (Ecclesiastes 12:3, 5, 7). This is a picture of the body of corruption. Its destiny is death, decay, and dissolution. But if we are to have bodies in Heaven, we must have bodies that are free from corruption. This is exactly the kind of body that Christ will give us when He comes. It was buried in corruption, but it will be raised in incorruption. We have some idea of an incorruptible body in the scene on the Mount of Transfiguration. Moses and Elijah both appeared with Christ. Moses had died fifteen hundred years before. Yet he was there recognizable in a glorious body. Elijah had been caught up to Heaven without dying about nine hundred years before, and he too was there in a glorified body. Our resurrection will clothe us with bodies where disease and sickness will never enter. No pain, no weakness, no fever will touch our resurrection bodies. "And God shall wipe away all tears from their eyes; and there shall be no more death, neither sorrow, nor crying, neither shall there be any more pain: for the former things are passed away" (Revelation 21:4).

From Dishonour To Glory

"It is sown in dishonour; it is raised in glory" (1 Corinthians 15:43).

The body that is put in the grave is sown in dishonour. The average Christian sadly neglects his body, failing to realize that it is the temple of the Holy Spirit. Proper care of the body is far more the exception than it is the rule. The bodies of some Christians have been broken and diseased by sin before the persons ever came to a knowledge of the truth. The drinking of intoxicating liquors, the use of tobacco, and other sins of the body have brought to the body dishonour. Some do not get enough rest, while others injure the body through laziness and inactivity. Some persons overeat regularly while others mistreat the body by not eating the right kind of food. It is the opinion of the writer that the majority of people are guilty of not giving the body its required care. It is sown in dishonour. But our resurrection bodies will be raised in glory. We shall be like Jesus, in the brightness of His glory. O glorious hope!

From Weakness to Power

"It is sown in weakness; it is raised in power" (1 Corinthians 15:43).

It is believed that the Apostle Paul was frail in body, afflicted with "a thorn in the flesh". Weak bodies have their limitations, and many of us can testify as to how the work of the Lord often is hampered by bodily limitations. The tasks we seek to perform become wearisome by reason of the infirmities of the flesh. But in Heaven we shall know nothing of physical weakness. The limitations of earth are not known in Heaven. What a glorious change that will be! Raised in power! Here on earth we find that the spirit sometimes is willing, but the flesh is weak. Some of God's choice saints cannot as much as attend a church service because of bodily affliction, but in Heaven all will have strong bodies. The new body will be a habitation from God, incorruptible, immortal, and powerful.

From the Natural To the Spiritual

"It is sown a natural body; it is raised a spiritual body" (1 Corinthians 15:44).

It must be clearly understood that the phrase "a spiritual body" does not so much as infer that the resurrection body will be a body without substance. The word "natural" is from a word used by the Greeks when they spoke of the soul of man. We pointed out earlier in this volume how that man was made of three component parts: body, soul, and spirit. In the physical he possesses world-consciousness through his five senses. With his soul, which is the seat of his emotions, he possesses self-consciousness, thereby having knowledge that he is a personality. By his spirit, he is enabled to know God and to worship and serve Him after his human spirit has been quickened by the Holy Spirit. Our bodies while on earth are natural or soulish bodies and are engaged chiefly with the activities and the environment of earth. By nature it becomes easily adjusted to work and play. The spiritual life is not absent altogether from man, but it occupies a small part of his time and energy as compared with his soul life.

When the resurrection body is called "a spiritual body," it is not meant that it will be composed of intangible substance. Robert S. Candlish has said: "The words natural and spiritual, as applied to the body, have respect not so much to the nature of the substance of which the body is composed, as to the uses or purposes which it is intended to serve." On earth we are occupied to a greater degree with the natural body, while in Heaven in our resurrection bodies we will be occupied with all that pertains to God and godliness. The spiritual life of man will prevail.

We might say that the body has two masters, a natural and a spiritual. Paul said: "When I would do good, evil is present with me" (Romans 7:21). The Apostle was truly God's child by the transforming power of the Holy Spirit, but the natural man was still very much alive and warring against the spiritual. And each of us knows too well what a barrier the natural man is! We are hindered by the attitude of the natural toward the spiritual. But in Heaven we shall be clothed with a resurrection body where the higher principles in man will predominate and the full tide of spiritual life will be in control.

In Heaven all will be incorrupt, immortal, glorious, powerful, and spiritual. Before the throne of God we will serve Him eternally in His temple. O glorious hope! O resurrection day!

CHAPTER SEVEN

THE FUTURE JUDGMENT OF THE BELIEVER

THE coming of Christ will be an occasion of jubilation for all saints. When the graves are opened and the dead in Christ shall rise first and the living saints shall be caught up together with them to meet the Lord in the air, it will be a time such as attends the meeting of a bride with her bridegroom.

Believers never need fear a condemnatory judgment for sin. For every Christian this judgment is already past. When Jesus comes again He will have in His body the marks of crucifixion, and this will prove that the penalty for sin has been paid in full. Our Lord reassures us by His own word: "Verily, verily, I say unto you, He that heareth My word, and believeth on Him that sent Me, hath everlasting life, *and shall not come into condemnation*; but is passed from death unto life" (John 5:24). To this the Apostle Paul adds: "There is therefore now no condemnation to them which are in Christ Jesus" (Romans 8:1). Our souls rest forever upon these eternal words of our God.

ALL MEN AND FALLEN ANGELS ARE TO BE JUDGED

Yet the Bible teaches clearly that all men, both living and dead, saved and unsaved, must give an account to Christ. The Apostle Peter, in his great sermon in the house of Cornelius, said "that it is He which was ordained of God to be the Judge of quick and dead" (Acts 10:42). Later, in his First Epistle, Peter wrote that the saints "shall give account to Him that is ready to judge the quick (the living) and the dead" (1 Peter 4:5). Those who were dead, those who have died since or will have died, and the living must give account to Jesus Christ who is ready to judge all men.

The Five Separate Future Judgments

Not all men will be judged at the same time and place. There are five future judgments. The first of these will be the judgment of the believer's works, called "The Judgment Seat of Christ". It is this judgment to which we shall give consideration in this chapter. But first, we shall outline the four future judgments that will follow the judgment of the believer's works.

The Judgment of Regathered Israel. In Daniel 12:1 this judgment is called "The Time of Jacob's Trouble". It will be the punishment of the Jews for their disobedience to God and their rejection of Jesus Christ. During the Tribulation Period and after the close of the present Age of Grace, Israel will pay for her sins, being afflicted with unprecedented misery and woe.

The Judgment of the Living Nations. At the end of the Tribulation Period, after Israel has been judged, the nations of the earth will be judged by Christ and His Church. This judgment will not be against individuals but against nations for their treatment of the Jewish people. "For, behold, in those days, and in that time, when I shall bring again the captivity of Judah and Jerusalem, I will also gather all nations, and will bring them down into the valley of Jehoshaphat, and will plead with them there for my people and for my heritage Israel, whom they have scattered among the nations, and parted my land" (Joel 3:1, 2).

The Judgment of Fallen Angels. This is the final judgment against Satan and other fallen angels who will be judged with him. Immediately after the one thousands years of the Kingdom Age, Satan and his hosts will meet their doom. "And the angels which kept not their first estate, but left their own habitation, He hath reserved in everlasting chains under darkness unto the judgment of the great day" (Jude 6). At that time we shall see the final fulfillment of that great prophecy in Genesis 3:15.

The Judgment of the Unbelieving Dead. This is called the Great White Throne Judgment. After the casting of Satan into Hell, the wicked dead will be raised to receive the final sentence of condemnation (Revelation 20:12-15). No believer will be judged at that day as the final judgment is reserved for all who rejected the Lord Jesus Christ on earth.

THE JUDGMENT SEAT OF CHRIST

The first future judgment derives its name from two passages where the term "Judgment Seat of Christ" appears—

> "For we shall all stand before the judgment seat of Christ" (Romans 14:10).
> "For we must all appear before the judgment seat of Christ" (2 Corinthians 5:10).

This judgment cannot be confused with either of the other judgments because the Holy Spirit used a Greek word to describe the Judgment Seat of Christ that is peculiar and different from the Greek words used in connection with other judgments. Here the word used is *bema*. It appears in classical Greek to identify the judge's seat in the arena of the Olympic games. The *bema* was the seat whereon the judge sat, not to punish contestants, but to present awards to the victors. When Christians stand before the *bema* of Christ, it will be for the express purpose of being rewarded according to their works. There is no idea of inflicting punishment.

1. *The Judge.* Our Lord Himself said: "The Father judgeth no man, but hath committed all judgment unto the Son" (John 5:22). The Apostle Paul said to

the Athenians that "God hath appointed a day, in the which He will judge the world in righteousness by that Man Whom He hath ordained; whereof He hath given assurance unto all men, in that He hath raised Him from the dead" (Acts 17:31). In this sense every judgment throne can be considered as the judgment seat of Christ, for, as the resurrected Son of God, He has been appointed by the Father to be the Judge of all. However, there is only one *bema*, a throne erected for Christ for the purpose of awarding the prizes or crowns to the victorious saints.

Since Christ is the Judge, and a time and place have been set for the judgment of believers, we are warned against any attempt at judging each other in this life. "Why dost thou judge thy brother? or why dost thou set at nought thy brother? for we shall all stand before the judgment seat of Christ" (Romans 14:10). We are not judges. Therefore we have no right to judge or to despise our brother. It is not possible for any of us to judge righteously and justly because we do not know the hearts of each other. Jesus warned His disciples: "Judge not, that ye be not judged"(Matthew 7:1). We must exercise a careful discrimination in all matters, but our attitude is to be without censoriousness. We are expected to use our reason and the powers of discernment, but never to avenge, condemn, nor damn another. Abraham Kuyper has said: "All human judgment remains imperfect. It can never fully satisfy our thirst after justice." A human tribunal cannot bring a just retribution upon those who have committed crimes in secret. Too frequently the guilty are set free and the innocent condemned. "Forget not your martyrs". Because of our limitations we come to wrong conclusions. Therefore we are to leave all judgment with the omniscient Judge who will judge righteously and accurately, but never falsely. When

Jesus comes, every Christian, dead or alive will be included in the great throng that will stand before the *bema* of Christ. We will be there, not merely as spectators or witnesses. The Holy Judge will not need anyone to witness. In that day His word shall stand. "He knew all men, and needed not that any should testify of man: for He knew what was in man" (John 2:24, 25).

2. *The Judged.* Only believers will appear before the Judgment Seat of Christ. In both verses where this judgment is mentioned (Romans 14:10; 2 Corinthians 5:10), the words are addressed to Christians only. All the wicked dead (unbelievers) will be judged at the Great White Throne after the one thousand years' reign of Christ on earth. But the subjects to whom the Apostle Paul addressed his messages when he said, "*We* must all appear," were exclusively the saints of whom Paul considered himself one. Someone will question the possibility of standing room for the countless millions of saints, or another may question the time element of such "an endlessly drawn out pronouncement of judgment upon so large a host of individuals". The Bible is silent on details as to the exact location of the place of judgment. Whether in Heaven or in the air we cannot tell. However, one thing is certain, as Henry W. Frost has said: "A divine judgment need not take long". It is absurd even to conceive of a problem of space when we think of the vast expanse in the heavens. "It is possible that this judgment of the saints will be instantaneous, and that each Christian will rise into the air to enter at once into his proper place and appointed rewarding". If there are problems regarding the exact location and the manner of this judgment, there are none regarding its certainty, "For *we must all appear* before the judgment seat of Christ".

The Christian's Works Will Be Tested

Let us pause to read carefully the Holy Spirit's message concerning Christian work and its rewards—

> "For we are labourers together with God: ye are God's husbandry, ye are God's building. According to the grace of God which is given unto me, as a wise masterbuilder, I have laid the foundation, and another buildeth thereon. But let every man take heed how he buildeth thereupon. For other foundation can no man lay than that is laid, which is Jesus Christ. Now if any man build upon this foundation gold, silver, precious stones, wood, hay, stubble; Every man's work shall be made manifest: for the day shall declare it, because it shall be revealed by fire; and the fire shall try every man's work of what sort it is. If any man's work abide which he hath built thereupon, he shall receive a reward. If any man's work shall be burned, he shall suffer loss: but he himself shall be saved; yet so as by fire" (1 Corinthians 3:9-15).

The great Apostle refers to himself and all of his fellow-workers as "labourers together with God". This is a wonderful truth when we realize that God does not actually need any one of us to do His work. It is not necessary that He should consider us at all to carry His Gospel, for He can carry out the whole plan of salvation without us. He could send His holy angels to spread redemption's message, or He could flash it across the skies to the visibility of every person in the universe, but He has chosen the believer to tell the story of His sovereign grace and matchless love.

The foundation for this work is already laid, "For other foundation can no man lay than that is laid, which is Jesus Christ" (verse 11). Now we are to build upon this foundation, and the work in which we engage ourselves must stand the test of the judgment seat of Christ if we are to receive a reward. "Every man's work shall be made manifest . . . and the fire shall try every man's work of what sort it is". Many Christians who have labored humbly and prayerfully in the Spirit will be rewarded, but that which was done in the energy of the flesh and which is merely called "Christian work" will be consumed by the fire of purging. "If a man's work abide, he shall receive a reward. If a man's work shall be burned, he shall suffer loss." "*We* shall be judged" according to the secret motives and the character of our work. If you cannot do all that you would like to do, be sure that whatever you do is of the right "sort." This means that if our work is of the right kind or character, we will receive a reward. Contrariwise, if what a believer does is not of the right character, "he shall suffer loss: but he himself shall be saved; yet so as by fire" (1 Corinthians 3:15).

In an interesting and instructive parable of our Lord recorded by Luke (Luke 18:11-27), we have a picture of this present age and the Christian's responsibility. "A certain nobleman went into a far country to receive for himself a kingdom, and to return. And he called his ten servants, and delivered them ten pounds, and said unto them, Occupy till I come". The ten pounds were divided equally among the ten servants, thus showing that each servant had an equal opportunity during the Lord's absence. To each of us has been committed the witness of Jesus Christ. We are to share in the opportunities and responsibilities of making Him known. Not one single Christian can say that he is not responsible for the spreading of the truth of the Gospel. During our Lord's absence we are to occupy till He comes, for He is coming again, as He said, to render to every man according to his deeds.

"When he was returned, having received the kingdom, then he commanded these servants to be called unto him, to whom he had given the money, that he might know how much every man had gained by trading". Here our Lord describes what will happen when He returns. All of us who are His shall be called unto Him to give an account of ourselves as to how we discharged our responsibilities during His absence. This is the Judgment Seat of Christ, and it will determine our position and service in the Millennial Kingdom. Recently in Philadelphia two men took the same examination with the understanding that the one receiving the highest grade would be appointed to the office of Chief of the Fire Bureau. It is by the same method of competitive examination in faithfulness that the saints will be appointed to rule with Christ. In the parable the servant who gained ten pounds was called "faithful", and was given authority over ten cities. Likewise the servant which gained five pounds was given authority over five cities. But the servant who returned his one pound having done nothing with it was sternly rebuked. The Lord said: "Take from him the pound, and give it to him that hath ten pounds".

When Jesus comes each believer will receive his or her just reward for service according to the measure and motive of our works. No rewards will be given by political preferment, but only in exact proportion to the genuine effort put forth. Other parables of our Lord which should be studied in connection with Christian service are the Unprofitable Servant (Luke 17:7-10), The Laborers in the Vineyard (Matthew 20:1-16), and The Talents (Matthew 25:14-30).

Saints Will Differ In Heaven

The Apostle Paul says: "There is one glory of the sun, and another glory of the moon, and another glory of the stars: for one star differeth from another star in glory. So also is the resurrection of the dead" (1 Corinthians 15:41, 42). Every Christian will be given a celestial body in the Resurrection, but these bodies will differ in the glory that each shall possess and enjoy in Heaven. Paul asks us to notice how the stars differ in glory, some shining with a greater brilliance than others. Then he concludes: "So also is the resurrection of the dead". All believers will have glorified bodies, but there will be difference in glory according to the measure of our diligence and devotedness to Christ and His work. I hold in my hand three coins. One is gold, one is silver, and the third is copper. All three bear the same inscription of the United States of America. However, the glory of the gold is one glory, the glory of the silver is a lesser glory, and the glory of the copper is yet a lesser glory than either the gold or the silver. So also is the resurrection of the dead. Each of the bodies of the saved will bear the glorified and heavenly mark of distinction, but the glory of some will differ from the glory of others. Our capacity to serve in Heaven we will take to Heaven with us when Jesus comes.

THE CROWNS OR REWARDS

"Behold, I come quickly: hold that fast which thou hast, that no man take thy crown" (Revelation 3:11).

"And, behold, I come quickly; and My reward is with Me, to give every man according as his work shall be" (Revelation 22:12).

The Judgment Seat of Christ will be a crowning day for those Christians who will receive rewards for their works. The New Testament teaches that these are called "crowns". There are five such "crowns" to be given.

The Incorruptible Crown. "And every man that striveth for the mastery is temperate in all things. Now they do it to obtain a corruptible crown; but we an incorruptible" (1 Corinthians 9:25). Here Paul has in mind the athlete in the Roman arena. Before the contest each participant practiced self-discipline, being temperate in all things. There were doubtless many pleasures and pastimes that the athletes might have entered into and enjoyed, but they denied themselves these things in order to do their best. A crown awaited the victor. The incorruptible crown for the Christian is the victor's crown for those who keep under the body and bring it into subjection. There are certain pleasures, worldly amusements, manners of dress, and uses of cosmetics that interfere with one's progress in spreading the Gospel and winning the lost to Christ. If I live victoriously over all things, "making no provision for the flesh to fulfill the lusts thereof," I shall gain the reward for a victorious life which is the Incorruptible Crown. If an athlete must subject himself to many months of rigid discipline and training to obtain a corruptible crown, how much more should we bring our bodies into subjection for a crown that is incorruptible!

The Crown of Rejoicing. "For what is our hope, or joy, or crown of rejoicing? Are not even ye in the presence of our Lord Jesus Christ at His coming? For ye are our glory and joy" (1 Thessalonians 2:19, 20). This is the soul-winner's crown. The first thing that a Christian should pray for and seek to cultivate is the desire, ability, and wisdom to win lost souls to Jesus Christ. Paul was confident that when he would stand before the Judgment Seat of Christ the Thessalonian converts would guarantee a crown for all those who shared in bringing them to Christ. Every time an individual is converted, there is joy in Heaven; but at the day of the giving of rewards the soul-winner will be exceeding joyful when those are presented to God whom he had won to Christ. What is our hope of reward as Christ's witnesses? The answer is in those who will be in Heaven because of our prayers, gifts, preaching, and personal work.

The Crown of Righteousness. "Henceforth there is laid up for me a crown of righteousness, which the Lord, the righteous judge, shall give me at that day: and not to me only, but unto them also that love His appearing" (2 Timothy 4:8). Here the character of the reward corresponds to the character of the Giver. Both are said to be righteous. The doctrine of our Lord's return is regarded very highly by God. In spite of the fact that Jesus said He would come again, there are many people who scoff at the thought of Christ's appearing. This and kindred truths have brought suffering and hardship, and in some cases death, to those who insisted on preaching and teaching them. But how wonderful to know that God has prepared a special reward for all who look for that blessed hope, who wait for His Son from Heaven, and who love His appearing!

The Crown of Life. "Blessed is the man that endureth temptation: for when he is tried, he shall receive the crown of life, which the Lord hath promised to them that love Him" (James 1:12).

"Fear none of those things which thou shalt suffer: behold, the devil shall cast some of you into prison, that ye may be tried; and ye shall have tribulation ten days: be thou faithful unto death, and I will give thee a crown of life" (Revelation 2:10).

The Crown of Life is reserved for those who have given their lives for the sake of the Gospel. Not all of our Lord's witnesses have been called to suffering and martyrdom. Not all would willingly pay with their lives to take the message of salvation to the lost. How thoughtful and just our heavenly Father was when He prepared a martyr's crown for those who suffer persecution for Christ's sake! Though some of us will not receive the Crown of Life, we will rejoice with those who refused to count the cost and have died proclaiming the Gospel of Christ.

The Crown of Glory. "Feed the flock of God which is among you, taking the oversight thereof, not by constraint, but willingly; not for filthy lucre, but of a ready mind; Neither as being lords over God's heritage, but being ensamples to the flock. And when the chief Shepherd shall appear, ye shall receive a crown of glory that fadeth not away. Likewise, ye younger, submit yourselves unto the elder. Yea, all of you be subject one to another, and be clothed with humility: for God resisteth the proud, and giveth grace to the humble" (1 Peter 5:2-5). There are many who have been called and ordained by God to preach and teach His Word. These are the under-shepherds who care for the flock of God during the absence of the Chief Shepherd. My brother-minister, let us give ourselves without ostentation to the care of the sheep of His pasture, for the crown of unfading glory awaits us in the day when the Chief Shepherd shall appear.

If there is to be joy and rejoicing for those who receive the crowns, surely there will be disappointment and sorrow for those who will not receive them. God keeps an exact record of the sins and works of His children. The record includes all of our motives and acts, our response to or our rejection of God's call to faithful stewardship and service. When an unfaithful Christian hears and sees the true record of his unfaithfulness; when he is reminded of the large sum of money he left behind, a portion of which could have been given to the spreading of the Gospel; when he sees how the cause of Christ has suffered because of his neglect and indifference; when a Christian who has wronged his brother and never repented of his sin sees that ugly deed dragged out of its hiding place, will that Christian be unmoved by the revealing of his empty and wasted life while on earth? Will there be no regret, no shame, no consternation? Listen once again to God's immortal declaration: "If a man's work shall be burned, he shall suffer . . ."

The story was told of a great fire in a city apartment house. The tenants had all been led to safety with the exception of one family on one of the upper floors. The mother, driven to frenzy by the terror that accompanied the flaming and smoke-filled room, leaped to safety into a fireman's net. But it was discovered that, in her befogged and delirious mind, she completely forgot her children who perished in the flames. She was saved as by fire, but she suffered great loss. May God grant that we should strive to labor in the light of that hour when all of our work shall be judged by Jesus Christ Himself and we shall be rewarded accordingly.

The Judgment Seat of Christ seems a necessity to the writer. Think of the believers, all members of the body of Christ, who are divided because of differences. In organizations, in churches, and in families I have seen Christians who are not on speaking terms. People who were at one time very close and intimate friends are now separated and a bitter feeling exists between them. Each blames the separation on the other, and they continue on, trying to serve the Lord, but their difference has not been adjusted. Now if our Lord returns before there is a reconciliation of such Christians here on earth, it is necessary that they get right with each other somewhere, for certainly they cannot continue on forever in holding hatred and animosity in their hearts. Heaven knows no such actions. Hatred and unforgiveness is sin. Yet there is no sin in Heaven. Hence the necessity of the Judgment Seat of Christ.

The Judgment Seat of Christ is necessary because not one believer has received his reward for any service he has renderd in this life. Often, and frequently at funerals, we hear it said that the departed one has gone to his eternal reward. This is not Scripturally correct. The departed saints are with the Lord, but not one has received his reward as yet. We are not rewarded one by one at death. None of the disciples nor the apostles has received his rewards yet, nor will he until Jesus comes back and all saints are gathered together. Jesus said to the Pharisee in whose house He had dined: "Thou shalt be blessed; for they cannot recompense thee: for thou shalt be recompensed at the resurrection of the just" (Luke 14:14).

Dear Christian, "Be ye steadfast, unmoveable, always abounding in the work of the Lord, forasmuch as ye know that your labor is not in vain in the Lord" (1 Corinthians 15:58). "For God is not unrighteous to forget your work and labour of love" (Hebrews 6:10). "And whatsoever ye do, do it heartily, as to the Lord, and not unto men; knowing that of the Lord ye shall receive the reward of the inheritance: for ye serve the Lord Christ" (Colossians 3:23, 24).

One final word! "And now, little children, abide in Him; that, when He shall appear, we may have confidence, and not be ashamed before Him at His coming" (1 John 2:28). Ashamed at His coming! What a sorry closing chapter for any believer's life! We shudder at the thought of being found in a theatre or a tavern, at a card game or some other worldly amusement when Jesus comes. How ashamed we will be if we are engaged in dishonest business, unclean conversation, or unholy living! Let us, with singleness of purpose, abandon ourselves to His perfect will for our lives so that we may hear Him say to us: "Well done".

CHAPTER EIGHT

THE ETERNAL PUNISHMENT
OF THE LOST

THIS chapter is an endeavor to write a statement of the most solemn doctrine in all the Bible. When I first attempted to preach on this subject some years ago, invariably I found myself asking God for tenderness in presenting it. Today I must confess that there still lingers an averseness on my part to declare that there is no hope that any measure of divine grace or mercy ever will be extended to one person after death, but that there is rather a fearful anticipation of retribution in the lake of fire. This averseness to assert the divine claims about Hell is not the result of waning convictions or of doubts concerning the reality and literalness of the everlasting misery of the unsaved. Contrariwise, the growing convictions and God-given confirmations of the endless agony of the wicked dead cause me to tremble at the horrible thought of damned souls in flames of torment forever.

HELL—AN UNPOPULAR SUBJECT

Furthermore, I am aware of the fact that this subject is an unpopular one. Since those memorable days when Jonathan Edwards preached that potent and moving sermon on "Sinners in the Hands of an Angry God", the doctrine of the eternal retribution of the lost has gradually gone into obscurity. A daily newspaper printed the following on May 29, 1944. "A Navy chaplain said today some naval officers forbade chaplains to tell their men they were in danger of hell. The chaplain, Frederick Volbeda, of Washington, a veteran of Pearl Harbor, said his own commanding officer once heard him preach repentance and actual punishment and swore he would 'have no hell-fire preaching on this ship' ". Chaplain Volbeda made his report at the 84th annual General Assembly of the Southern Presbyterian Church.

When Irvin S. Cobb, the internationally famous humorist and writer, died in March 1944, he referred to Heaven as "a powerfully dull place, populated to a considerable and uncomfortable degree by prigs, time servers and unpleasantly aggressive individuals", and then he added that "hell may have a worse climate but undoubtedly the company is sprightlier". Of course Cobb did not believe in Hell, for he insisted that those in charge of his burial "avoid reading the so-called Christian burial service, which, in view of the language employed in it, I regard as one of the most cruel and paganish things inherited by our forbears from our remote pagan ancestry. Instead, let the 23rd Psalm be read. This has no threat of eternal hell fire".

Irvin Cobb was doubtless a success as a humorist, but no amount of jocose treatment of Hell can deliver him from the anguish and agony of his soul today. The best this wit and humorist could say about our Lord Jesus Christ was that He was "the greatest gentleman that ever lived". To all such flattery and humanism our Lord only answers: "Ye must be born again". On this vital and eternal issue Cobb declared himself. If he died denying every fundamental doctrine of the Christian faith, how solemn will be his day of accounting for casting such aspersions. God brands all who reject and ridicule His Word as "raging waves of the sea foaming out their own shame, . . . to whom is reserved the blackness of darkness forever" (Jude 13). Some day the tables will be turned, and "He that sitteth in the heavens shall laugh" (Psalm 2:4).

Our hearts go out in sympathy and pity for Cobb and the millions like him who died unbelievers and passed consciously into an endless eternity and the hell fire they scoffed and denied.

Mr. Cobb requested that at his funeral the Twenty-Third Psalm be read because it contains "no threat of eternal hell fire". We do not propose a debate on the theological content of this best loved Psalm of David, but we can say without fear of contradiction that Cobb's knowledge of the Bible was the result of a prejudiced investigation, to say the least. The Author of the Shepherd-Psalm is also the Author of all that the world knows about the future life, and eschatology of the Holy Scriptures is not silent on the doctrine of the eternal retribution of the unbelieving and wicked dead in a place of torment.

FALSE THEORIES

Many conflicting theories have been formed regarding this subject. Of course, those mentioned under the above heading are human theories that have not the support of the Word of God. Here we can do little more than make a passing reference to these man-made ideas. These are: *Conditional Immortality, Universalism* and the *Restoration Theory*.

Conditional Immortality. This theory is built on the error that all who do not receive everlasting life will die as the animals and be annihilated or wiped out of existence. It contends that immortality is conditional upon receiving the gift of everlasting life. If anyone dies not having the gift of everlasting life he shall not be punished with everlasting torment. He shall be annihilated.

Universalism. The universalistic theory holds the idea of universal redemption. For example, a certain number of Scripture references are used to prove that Christ died for all men alike. Therefore all men alike shall be saved in the end. Universalism uses such texts as Paul's when he said: "We preach, warning every man, and teaching every man in all wisdom; that we may present every man perfect in Christ Jesus" (Colossians 1:28). Certainly the Apostle could not have meant that he expected every man that ever came into the world to be made perfect in Christ. The words "every man" could refer only to those to whom Paul addressed his Epistle; namely, "To the saints and faithful brethren in Christ" (1:2). This theory does not deny that all men are lost by sin, but it contends that all men will finally be saved and enter into everlasting life. Universalism falls when it overlooks the Biblical fact that salvation and everlasting life are applied to no one apart from his personal acceptance of it as a divinely bestowed gift to "whosoever will".

The Restoration Theory. This view, called by some, *Restitutionism*, appeals to the universalist, in that it does not deny that all men are lost, but that sometime, somewhere, all creation (including Satan and the fallen angels) will be restored or reconciled to God. Being contrary to reason and common sense, the average person labels this view as preposterous. But let us look at two texts that are used to form the basis of the false view of Restitutionism. The words of our Lord are quoted: "And I, if I be lifted up from the earth, will draw *all men* unto Me" (John 12:32). We must exercise care that these words of Christ do not lead us to believe the heretical teaching of Restitutionism. Our Saviour never meant that all men finally shall be saved by His crucifixion. Dr. A. C. Gaebelein in his commentary on "The Gospel of John" says: "The analogy of other texts shows plainly that the only reasonable sense is, that Christ's crucifixion would have a 'drawing' influence on men of all nations, Gentiles as well as Jews". But it is quite possible also that this verse has a future application. In the preceding verse (31) which was given in connection with verse thirty-two, Jesus spoke of the future when "the prince of this world shall be cast out". Of a truth, in that day "all men" will be drawn unto Him.

Another favorite text used by the Restitutionists is one of Peter's statements given in his second sermon after Pentecost. The Apostle said:

> "Repent ye therefore, and be converted, that your sins may be blotted out, when the times of refreshing shall come from the presence of the Lord; And he shall send Jesus Christ, which before was preached unto you: Whom the heaven must receive until the times of restitution of all things, which God hath spoken by the mouth of all his holy prophets since the world began" (Acts 3:19-21).

Again the teachers of this false doctrine have seized upon a phrase and have deliberately torn it from its context to make it fit their scheme of thought. The phrase "restitution of all things" cannot be interpreted correctly if applied to any other than the house of Israel. Remember, it is to Israel that Peter is addressing his message. His introductory statement was: "Ye men of Israel" (vs. 12). It is the restitution of all things for Israel when Christ comes to restore the nation to which the apostle is referring. Furthermore, it is to be the "restitution of all things, which God hath spoken *by the mouth of all His holy prophets.*" Immediately we are limited in defining Peter's statement, for we must confine it to the restitution (or restoration) of which the prophets spoke. Frequently the prophets wrote of the restoration of Israel to the land of Palestine, but nowhere in the prophetic writings have we ever come across so much as an inference that the wicked dead ever will be saved.

Restitutionism depends largely upon that mighty statement uttered by the Apostle Paul in Philippians 2:10, 11, "That at the name of Jesus every knee should bow, of things in heaven, and things in earth, and things under the earth; and that every tongue should confess that Jesus Christ is Lord, to the glory of God the Father". This passage means that all creation, whether animate or inanimate, in heaven, on earth, or under the earth, will confess (or publicly declare) and thereby agree to the testimony that God the Father has given of His Son. There is not the slightest indication that all men who acknowledge the authority of Christ *must* be saved or that they *will* be saved. While our Lord was here on earth the demons frequently acknowledged His authority (See Mark 1:24, 34; 3:11, 12), and we know that everlasting fire is prepared for the Devil and his angels (Matthew 25:41).

ARGUING AGAINST HELL FROM THE LOVE OF GOD

We hear it said often that God is too tender, kind, and forgiving to allow men to suffer in Hell. Pleading the love and pity of God, men insist that He would not allow His creatures to perish. There are many beautiful and sentimental sayings about the love of God that are quoted to support the view that He would not allow one soul to suffer torment in eternity. But we dare never lose sight of the fact that one's escape from Hell is not dependent upon the love of God but upon the repentance and faith of each individual person. God is love, to be certain, but man also has a free will. Men are not doomed and damned to Hell by God, but they go there because they have willfully rejected God's only way of escape from sin's penalty, saving faith in the Lord Jesus Christ. God was love in the Old Testament times, and yet the children of Israel were punished for their sins. God is love now, but he does not open the doors of penal institutions to deliver those who are being punished for their crimes. It is but the fair treatment of society to protect it against the persistent wrong doings of the criminal, and certainly Heaven would not be safe nor desirable if there were no protection against sin and crime. It would seem to the writer that God owes it to the faithful believers that the wicked be separated from them in Heaven. It would be an insult to the justice and honor of God were He to allow the unrighteous and unholy rejectors of Jesus Christ to share eternally the abode and "the things which God hath prepared for them that love Him" (1 Corinthians 2:9).

The natural and inevitable consequence of sin is punishment. Proper punishment of a child does not derogate from the love of the parent. Sin condemns just as surely as fire burns, and God is justified in putting into effect the immortal law that "whatsoever a man soweth, that shall he also reap" (Galatians 6:7).

HELL—A LITERAL PLACE OF FUTURE PUNISHMENT

Some people engage themselves in much wishful thinking about Hell. It has been said that the fires of Hell mean the torments of conscience. Others say that Hell is simply the grave. We do not question that the torments of conscience will be included in the eternal punishment of the lost, though Hell will not be the torments of conscience only. But we cannot agree at all with those who teach that Hell is simply the grave. One must be either a deceiver or an illiterate to say that Hell is the grave. When the unsaved rich man died he went to Hell, and cried: "I am tormented in this flame" (Luke 16:24). Certainly he was not merely in the grave. He had five brothers whom he desired to be saved lest they also should come to that place of torment. Now if his five brothers would have repented and become saved, their conversion could not have kept them from the grave, for "it is appointed unto men once to die" (Hebrews 9:27). Repentance and conversion will keep one from Hell but never from the grave. The bodies of all men, excepting those believers who are alive when Christ comes, will return to the dust. Hell is not the grave. The body of the rich man was dead, but that man knew that his soul was in a literal place and not merely in a spiritual state.

Notice the use of the word "fire" which denotes that the fire of Hell is as literal as the place itself. Repeatedly our Lord and the apostles spoke of the fire of Hell.

> "But I say unto you, That whosoever is angry with his brother without a cause shall be in danger of the judgment: and whosoever shall say to his brother, Raca, shall be in danger of the council; but whosoever shall say, Thou fool, shall be in danger of hell fire" (Matthew 5:22).
>
> "Every tree that bringeth not forth good fruit is hewn down, and cast into the fire" (Matthew 7:19).
>
> "The Son of man shall send forth his angels, and they shall gather out of his kingdom all things that offend, and them which do iniquity; And shall cast them into a furnace of fire: there shall be wailing and gnashing of teeth" (Matthew 13:41, 42).
>
> "Wherefore if thy hand or thy foot offend thee, cut them off, and cast them from thee: it is better for thee to enter into life halt or maimed, rather than having two hands or two feet to be cast into everlasting fire. And if thine eye offend thee, pluck it out, and cast it from thee: it is better for thee to enter into life with one eye, rather than having two eyes to be cast into hell fire" (Matthew 18:8, 9).

"Then shall he say also unto them on the left hand, Depart from me, ye cursed, into everlasting fire, prepared for the devil and his angels" (Matthew 25:41).

"Where their worm dieth not, and the fire is not quenched" (Mark 9:44).

"And he cried and said, Father Abraham, have mercy on me, and send Lazarus, that he may dip the tip of his finger in water, and cool my tongue; for I am tormented in this flame" (Luke 16:24).

"In flaming fire taking vengeance on them that know not God, and that obey not the gospel of our Lord Jesus Christ" (2 Thessalonians 1:8).

"And the angels which kept not their first estate, but left their own habitation, he hath reserved in everlasting chains under darkness unto the judgment of the great day. Even as Sodom and Gomorrah, and the cities about them in like manner, giving themselves over to fornication, and going after strange flesh, are set forth for an example, suffering the vengeance of eternal fire" (Jude 6, 7)

"The same shall drink of the wine of the wrath of God, which is poured out without mixture into the cup of his indignation; and he shall be tormented with fire and brimstone in the presence of the holy angels, and in the presence of the Lamb" (Revelation 14:10).

"Therefore shall her plagues come in one day, death, and mourning, and famine; and she shall be utterly burned with fire: for strong is the Lord God who judgeth her" (Revelation 18:8).

"And the beast was taken, and with him the false prophet that wrought miracles before him, with which he deceived them that had received the mark of the beast, and them that worshipped his image. These both were cast alive into a lake of fire burning with brimstone" (Revelation 19:20).

"And the devil that deceived them was cast into the lake of fire and brimstone, where the beast and the false prophet are, and shall be tormented day and night for ever and ever" (Revelation 20:10).

"And death and hell were cast into the lake of fire. This is the second death. And whosoever was not found written in the book of life was cast into the lake of fire" (Revelation 20:14, 15).

"But the fearful, and unbelieving, and the abominable, and murderers, and whoremongers, and sorcerers, and idolaters, and all liars, shall have their part in the lake which burneth with fire and brimstone: which is the second death" (Revelation 21:8).

You may study these statements and believe them, or else you may pass them by. You may believe that the Bible is for today, or else you may laugh at it as a bit of obsolete dogma. But today you are face to face with eternal statements in the Word of God which will survive the heavens and the earth. Your unbelief cannot disprove nor alter them. When the resurrected physical bodies of the unbelievers of every age leave the Judgment of the Great White Throne, they will go into a literal Hell of fire.

And be sure that the body will share with the soul in its suffering. Jesus said: "Marvel not at this: for the hour is coming, in the which all that are in the graves shall hear his voice, And shall come forth; they that have done good, unto the resurrection of life; and they that have done evil, unto the resurrection of damnation" (John 5:28, 29). May we ask what part of man is in the grave? We all agree that it is his body. Therefore we can depend on Christ's statement that that part of man that is buried in the grave will come forth to be damned eternally.

WILL FUTURE PUNISHMENT BE ENDLESS?

At death the eternal state of each person is immutably fixed. The words "eternal", "everlasting", "for ever", and "for ever and ever" express endless duration. The New Testament use of these expressions denotes eternity.* It is unreasonable to assume that there is an eternal Heaven but not an eternal Hell. Eternal punishment is as much a truth of God's Word as is the eternal rewards for the righteous. Jesus said: "And these shall go away into *everlasting* punishment: but the righteous into life *eternal*" (Matthew 25:46). The life of the righteous is everlasting, but so is the punishment of the wicked everlasting. The Bible says that salvation is *eternal* (Hebrews 5:9), life is *eternal* (John 6:54), redemption is *eternal* (Hebrews 9:12), and the inheritance of the saints is *eternal* (Hebrews 9:15). But it says also that the fire of Hell is *eternal* and *everlasting* (Matthew 18:8; Jude 7); the chains of Hell are *everlasting* (Jude 6); the blackness of darkness is *for ever* (Jude 13), and the torment is *for ever and ever* (Revelation 20:10). The punishment of the wicked and the life of the righteous are for equal duration, "for ever and ever".

WHERE IS HELL?

Here we cannot be dogmatic. This question cannot be answered fully. Geographically Hell cannot be located. The old theory that is held by many is that Hell is in the heart of the earth. A brief article appeared in "Moody Monthly" (July, 1940) in which the author sought to locate Hell. The following is a brief summary of that article.

It is clear that Hell is not in this earth. The Apostle Peter speaks of the day when the earth is to be dissolved by fire—

> "The earth also and the works that are therein shall be burned up. Seeing then that all these things shall be dissolved. . . . Nevertheless

* See an excellent book on the subject entitled "The Bible: Its Hell and Its Ages" by T. J. McCrossan, Seattle, Washington.

we, according to His promise, look for new heavens and a new earth wherein dwelleth righteousness" (2 Peter 3:10-13).

We are not persisting in this view of the geographical location of Hell, for the Bible gives us no positive declarative statement of its situation. Where this outer darkness is, where the endless fire is, where Hell is we do not know, nor must we know. It is sufficient to say that Hell is a prepared place, and experientially it is at the end of every unsaved sinner's life.

> "Come, sinners, seek His grace
> Whose wrath ye cannot bear;
> Flee to the shelter of His Cross,
> And find salvation there."

CHAPTER NINE

HEAVEN—THE HOME OF THE REDEEMED

H EAVEN! A comforting word is this! But who among us mortal creatures can envision its blessed reality? Neither the artist's brush, the sculptor's chisel, nor the theologian's exegesis can depict the things which God hath prepared for them who love Him. The wonder, the glory, and the effulgence of the home of the redeemed will be seen only through the eyes of our glorified bodies when we awake in Christ's likeness. "Now we see through a glass, darkly; but then face to face: now I know in part; but then shall I know even as also I am known" (1 Corinthians 13:12). Still we are not left alone to grope in dark ignorance. A foretaste of glory divine has been preserved for us upon the pages of God's eternal and unerring Word.

Is it not strange that we do not take up the Bible to study more about the abode of the blessed dead who die in the Lord? Should not we ourselves become better acquainted with our future home? What a pitiable plight would be ours if the Christian's hope of Heaven were but a hallucination! How dark would be the future if what we have been taught about Heaven were delusive and deceptive! But we can know the truth from God's Word and we can be certain that the descriptions of the Christian's future home are not fraudulent. Some years ago I was lured to an undesirable vacation spot by grossly exaggerated statements that spoke of refinement. Upon arriving I discovered that the town and its environment in no way tallied with the advertising. You can imagine how great was my disappointment. But the infallibility of the Holy Scriptures assures us of no disappointments in Heaven. We may be correctly informed by a careful study of what God says about it.

D. L. Moody told of an acquaintance whose only child had died. The accompanying sorrow was so great that his heart was almost broken by it. Before he suffered this loss, he had never given serious thought to life after death. Shortly after the child had been buried the friends and relatives of the man were surprised to see the deep interest he was showing in the Bible. He read it continually. When someone asked him about his sudden interest in the sacred Book, he answered that he was trying to find out something about the place where his boy had gone. He had come to the only source of satisfaction and reliable information. An instant after death the departed saint will know more about Heaven than all of the saints here on earth. But until we are called Home to be with the Lord, our knowledge is confined to what the Holy Spirit has revealed to us in the Bible.

THERE IS A PLACE CALLED HEAVEN

Some general ideas that are held about Heaven are not found in the Word of God. Because Heaven is beyond the limits of our vision many people regard it as merely a sphere of life, or a state independent of locality. But Heaven is a place. It was the dwelling *place* of Christ before His Incarnation. He said: "I came down from Heaven" (John 6:38). Heaven was also the place to which He ascended after His Resurrection. Luke says: "While He blessed them, He was parted from them, and carried up into Heaven" (Luke 24:51). It is the place where the glory and power of God are set forth. Jesus is there now, "set (or seated) on the right hand of the throne of the Majesty in the heavens" (Hebrews 8:1). Our Lord said: "I go to prepare a place for you" (John 14:2). When Jesus went away He must have gone somewhere, to a place. Therefore, we are not flattering ourselves with an unfounded hope that makes dying easier but that deceives us at the last. Some scientists have concluded that because Heaven could not be found, there is no such place. But the great expanse of the Almighty God is not within the measuring lines of man. True, the astronomer has located the North Star over 400,-000,000,000 miles away, but neither is that far when one reckons distance with God. We believe in the Biblical idea of Heaven as a definite, tangible place.

WHERE IS HEAVEN?

The Bible mentions three heavens: the aerial, the sidereal, and the celestial. First there is the atmospheric or aerial heavens where the birds fly. This is visible to the naked eye and is mentioned by Jeremiah where he said: "The birds of the heavens have fled" (Jeremiah 4:25). Next, there are the stellar or sidereal heavens from which shine the stars and constellations. Isaiah speaks of the Day of the Lord when "the stars of heaven and the constellations thereof shall not give their light" (Isaiah 13:10). Finally, there is the third Heaven, the celestial or "the Heaven of heavens" (2 Chronicles 6:18). "For Christ is not entered into the holy places made with hands, which are figures of the true; but into Heaven itself, now to appear in the presence of God for us" (Hebrews 9:24). Jesus said: "Let your light so shine before men, that they may see your good works and glorify your Father which is in Heaven" (Matthew 5:16). Here our Lord was referring to the third Heaven, and He says the Father is there.

When the believer dies he is "absent from the body, and present with the Lord" (2 Corinthians 5:8). He enters immediately into Heaven itself and is at home with the Lord.

But do we know the location of the third Heaven (called Paradise) where God, Christ, the unfallen angels, and the disembodied spirits of the believing dead are? In other words, exactly where is Heaven? If this question were asked of a small child, the answer doubtless would come back in the form of a finger pointing up, and perhaps the accompanying words, "Up there." Heaven to almost everyone is "up." Karl G. Sabiers asks: "Which way is 'up'? If we say it is in the direction at right angles with the earth's surface wherever we may happen to be, then it would be in a different direction from every point on the earth. From North America and from China it would be in exactly opposite directions. According to this, 'up' would be everywhere in general and nowhere in particular." When Satan rebelled against God, he said: "I will ascend into Heaven, I will exalt my throne above the stars of God; and I will sit upon the mount of congregation, *in the uttermost parts of the north*" (Isaiah 14:13 R.V.). No matter on what part of the earth one is standing, north will always be "up." When the prophet Ezekiel got his vision from the Lord, he wrote: "And I looked, and, behold, a whirlwind came out of the north" (Ezekiel 1:4). It would seem reasonable to conclude that Heaven is somewhere in the northern heavens beyond the reach of the astronomer's powerful telescope.

CHRISTIANS ARE CITIZENS OF HEAVEN

"For our citizenship is in Heaven; whence also we wait for a Saviour, the Lord Jesus Christ" (Philippians 3:20 R.V.). When Paul wrote this Epistle, Philippi was a Greek city but a colony of Rome, her citizens possessing Roman citizenship. The commonwealth of which the saints in Philippi were citizens had its fixed location in Rome. The Apostle Paul used this fact to illustrate to the believers their heavenly citizenship with its privileges and responsibilities. They were a heavenly people with a heavenly citizenship. Though they dwelt on earth, the commonwealth and the Sovereign of which the saints were citizens and subjects had its fixed location in Heaven. What was true of the saints at Philippi then is true of all believers. We were born from above. Ours is a heavenly destiny, and we are to live heavenly lives while we sojourn in a foreign land. As a heavenly people it is our privilege and responsibility to live a heavenly life on earth.

The Apostle Peter wrote: "Dearly beloved, I beeseech you as *strangers* and *pilgrims,* abstain from fleshly lusts, which war against the soul" (1 Peter 2:11). As strangers and pilgrims we are living in a temporary dwelling beside natives of a foreign land. Jesus Christ is our Sovereign. One day He will come back for us and take us to our native Home, changing our bodies of humiliation like to the body of His glory. The curse of sin has humiliated these physical bodies of ours, but we are to abstain from fleshly lusts and live the same holy life here that we would were we at home in our native Land. The Christian has a temporary home in a territory ruled by Satan, but he is not to subject himself to the god of this world. We must remain true to our Sovereign, "considering the High Priest of our profession. Christ Jesus," for we have become "partakers of the heavenly calling" (Hebrews 3:1).

Is the Present Heaven the Final Abode of the Saints?

There are several verses of Scripture that have confused not a few students of the Bible on this question. The following verses have led some to believe that the earth and the heavens that now are will one day be annihilated.

> "Of old hast thou laid the foundation of the earth: and the heavens are the work of thy hands. They shall perish, but thou shalt endure: yea, all of them shall wax old like a garment; as a vesture shalt thou change them, and they shall be changed" (Psalm 102:25, 26).
>
> "And all the host of heaven shall be dissolved, and the heavens shall be rolled together as a scroll: and all their host shall fall down, as the leaf falleth off from the vine, and as a falling fig from the fig tree" (Isaiah 34:4).
>
> "But the day of the Lord will come as a thief in the night; in the which the heavens shall pass away with a great noise, and the elements shall melt with fervent heat, and the earth also and the works that are therein shall be burned up. Seeing then that all these things shall be dissolved, what manner of persons ought ye to be in all holy conversation and godliness, Looking for and hasting unto the coming of the day of God, wherein the heavens being on fire shall be dissolved, and the elements shall melt with fervent heat? Nevertheless we, according to his promise, look for new heavens and a new earth, wherein dwelleth righteousness" (2 Peter 3:10-13).
>
> "And the world passeth away, and the lust thereof: but he that doeth the will of God abideth for ever" (1 John 2:17).
>
> "And I saw a great white throne, and him that sat on it, from whose face the earth and the heaven fled away; and there was found no place for them" (Revelation 20:11).

"And I saw a new heaven and a new earth:
for the first heaven and the first earth were
passed away; and there was no more sea"
(Revelation 21:1).

From these inspired statements of Peter and John
some have adopted the view that the present abode of
the righteous dead is to be burned up, reduced to
ashes, and an entirely new dwelling place created for
all of the saved. The writer finds difficulty in reconcil-
ing this teaching with other Scriptures. The Psalmist
testified: "Thy faithfulness is unto all generatons:
Thou hast established the earth, and it abideth"
(Psalm 119:90). It is written: "One generation passeth
away, and another generation cometh: but the earth
abideth forever" (Ecclesiastes 1:4). Here the teaching
appears to be that the creation of God will not be
annihilated, for He has said that it abides forever.
How, then, are we to understand this seeming contradiction? How can Heaven and earth be destroyed and
yet abide forever?

After the Millennium and the final judgment of
Satan the heavens and the earth will be thoroughly
purged by fire. This does not mean that the old heavens
and the old earth are to be completely consumed and
reduced to ashes. Neither is there any indication that
the new heaven and the new earth are to be entirely
new planets. The old world probably will be destroyed
by fire in the same sense that God destroyed it with
water in Noah's day, "Whereby the world that then
was, being overflowed with water, *perished*" (2 Peter
3:6). The world of Noah's day was not annihilated.
Geologists agree to the fact that the present world
shows evidence of being visited by a flood between
five and six thousand years ago. When we read in
Scripture that unbelievers shall "perish" (Luke 13:3,
5, 35), and be "destroyed" (Leviticus 23:30; Matthew

10:28), there is no thought of their being annihilated; for we have seen in two previous chapters how that both soul and body will exist in endless consciousness. But we do see an instructive parallel between the judgment of the earth by fire and the judgment of the lost by fire. Both are said to be "destroyed." Yet neither will be annihilated. We encounter no problem here when we think how the primitive earth which was made void by Satan (Genesis 1:2) was restored again by God and made new in the time of Adam and Eve.

It appears that the great conflagration, the flames and the melting, suggest the idea of purifying. There will be a new creation just as each believer who is born again is said to be a new creation. "Wherefore if any man is in Christ, he is a new creature (or a new creation): the old things are passed away: behold, they are become new" (2 Corinthians 5:17 R.V.). He is "created in Christ Jesus" (Ephesians 2:10). The new birth does not render inactive or annihilate the old nature. The child of God becomes a partaker of the New Nature which is divine, and all stain is purged by the Blood of Christ. Just exactly how God will bring to pass the purifying of the old heavens and the earth and make the new we do not know. But we are certain that they will pass through a molten ball of fire, and will come forth from that baptism of judicial fire clean and holy. Every stain of sin, every evidence of evil will be wiped out in that day.

We question the idea of the third Heaven being burned, for no purging or purifying is needed there. However, at the end of the day of the Lord, the earth and the heavens that surround it along with all the works of man will be consumed even as fire purifies gold. Then shall we have "a new heaven and a new earth" (Revelation 21:1)—not new in the sense of just coming into existence, but new in its renovation, transformation, and fixtures.

OUR HOME OVER THERE

When our Lord was here upon earth, He said to His disciples: "I go to prepare a place for you" (John 14:2). He was thinking of His Death, Resurrection, and Ascension into Heaven itself in the presence of the Father. The dwelling of God always has been a stately abode. Jesus describes it as a place of "many mansions," one Heaven divided into many rooms. The desire of the heavenly Bridegroom is to make ready a room for each of His redeemed ones. This He has been doing, and it was the unique privilege of the Apostle John to get a glimpse of the final abode of the righteous. Since we have a divine revelation of our heavenly Home presented to us by the Holy Spirit, we are assured of the accuracy of every description that He has given.

John says: "I saw a new heaven and a new earth . . . the holy city, new Jerusalem, coming down from God out of heaven, prepared as a bride adorned for her husband" (Revelation 21:1, 2). We are being introduced here to a place of absolute perfection and of eternal immutability, the home of the saved of all ages. It is called "the holy city" (Revelation 21.2; 22:19), for in it every person and every thing will echo the glory and the holiness of God. All powers of evil and all unbelievers will have been cast into the lake of fire forever. This means that every possibility of sin will have been expelled. When Jesus said He was going to prepare a place for us, it would be just such a place as this that one would expect the holy Son of God, the divine Architect, to build. No mere mortal hands could be employed in the construction of the Holy City. It must be of heavenly origin and construction.

The fellowship in Heaven will surpass anything that we have known on earth. Up there "God is with men; He will dwell with them, and God Himself shall be with them." We shall enter into a fellowship with the triune God that is utterly unknown on earth. Men dwelling with *"God Himself"!* Could anything be higher and more glorious? Then we will know the blessed reality of the words of Christ, where He said: "Blessed are the pure in heart: for they shall see God" (Matthew 5:8). In addition to having fellowship with "God Himself," Father, Son and Holy Spirit, we will commune with the "innumerable company of angels, the general assembly and church of the firstborn, and to the spirits of just men made perfect" (Hebrews 12:22-24). What a fellowship! What a joy divine!

Heaven will bring permanent relief from all of the ills of earth. It is written of the redeemed that in Heaven "God shall wipe away all tears from their eyes." I have dried the tears of my own children many times, but I have discovered my inability to stop the tears. When I feel that I have succeeded, I find that more tears begin to flow. The fountain of grief has been flowing perennially on earth since the dawn of the human race, and every earthly power has been limited in binding up broken hearts and assuaging the sorrows of man. But God is able. And how our hearts yearn for that glad occasion when the loving and almighty hand of our heavenly Father shall wipe away, once for all, every tear. The tears that flow from "sorrow," "crying," and "pain" shall be dried forever, for these things are not known in the land of pure delight. Earth's grief is forever gone and along with it is the extirpation of every cause.

In Heaven there will be "no more death." One cannot read the newspaper at home or walk the city streets without seeing our common enemy death. The hearse, the crepe, the undertaker, the graveyard, the stonecutter all seek to remind us that we are on the waiting list for death and the grave. But believe along with me the divine record that God has arranged a time when death itself shall die. Then shall be brought to pass the saying that is written, "Death is swallowed up in victory."

Heaven is revealed as a place of activity. John saw how that in the New Jerusalem "His servants shall serve Him" (Revelation 22:3). While it is true that Heaven is a place of rest, "a rest for the people of God," it will not be the rest of inactivity or idleness. We will not merely lounge within the pearly gates to gaze forever on the eternal beauty of our heavenly home. It is not the unwarranted view inscribed on a grave—

> "Don't weep for me now, don't weep for me ever;
> For I'm going to do nothing forever and ever".

Heaven would soon become monotonous if such were true. The saints "shall serve Him day and night in His temple" (Revelation 7:15), says John. When the Bible records the work of God in creation, it says: "And on the seventh day God ended His work which He had made; and He rested on the seventh day from all the work which He had made" (Genesis 2:2). Does this mean that God has been inactive and idle since creation? Most assuredly not! Jesus said: "My Father worketh hitherto, and I work" (John 5:17). By no means does the "rest" of the redeemed mean idleness. In Heaven we shall serve Him unhampered by earth's enemies and limitations, without painful stress and strain and sweat. "And what will we be doing?" someone asks. David said: "In Thy presence is fulness of joy; at Thy right hand there are pleasures for evermore" (Psalm 16:11). For one thing, we will enjoy to the full our blessed relationship with God. On earth we are hampered by so many things. The Apostle John realized that believers were enjoying merely a measure of that which God had for them. He wrote: "These things write we unto you, that your joy may be full" (1 John 1:4). In Heaven the joys and pleasures of our union with Jesus Christ will be appreciated and apprehended to the full, unhindered by the disturbing and distracting things on earth.

In Revelation 4:10, 11 we are clearly shown that in Heaven, we will worship our Lord and cast our crowns before His throne. On earth He is not worshipped and adored as He should be. Our so-called worship is sometimes no worship at all. How often we have gone through the motions when our hearts were not right! We enthrone self and steal the crowns to boast of what we have done. But yonder in the Land of pure delight, in our glorified state, we shall give Him our all. How these thoughts of our future home and its varied spheres of activity should encourage us to more zealous and diligent service during earth's pilgrimage! There is much about our heavenly activity that we do not know in detail now, but in that day we shall know even as we are known. But we know that we shall be engaged with Him who has redeemed us and brought us to our eternal dwelling place.

Babies in Heaven?

Jesus said:

> "At the same time came the disciples unto Jesus, saying, Who is the greatest in the kingdom of heaven? And Jesus called a little child unto him, and set him in the midst of them, And said, Verily I say unto you, Except ye be converted, and become as little children, ye shall not enter into the kingdom of heaven. Whosoever therefore shall humble himself as this little child, the same is greatest in the kingdom of heaven" (Matthew 18:1-4).
>
> "Even so it is not the will of your Father which is in heaven, that one of these little ones should perish" (Matthew 18:14).
>
> "But Jesus said, Suffer little children, and forbid them not, to come unto me: for of such is the kingdom of heaven" (Matthew 19:14).

Many able and well known Bible scholars have held the view that in Heaven there will be more occupants than in Hell. They base their belief on the fact that so many countless millions of children have died before reaching the age of accountability. It seems hardly possible that one of these little ones should ever be lost. Certainly they are not *saved,* that is, by believing in the Lord Jesus Christ (Acts 16:31). But it seems Scriptural and reasonable to conclude that all children who are not able to decide this issue for themselves are divinely *safe.*

Christian parents should, by daily prayer, the reading of the Scriptures, church attendance, and an exemplary life seek to lead their children who have arrived at an age of accountability to a saving knowledge of the Lord Jesus Christ. The thought of my being in Heaven while my children are lost in Hell would make me tremble. Let us make our first aim and duty the salvation of our children so that in Heaven the family circle will be unbroken. *See pages 114 and 115.*

CHAPTER TEN

SHALL WE KNOW EACH OTHER IN HEAVEN?

THE profoundness of the subject of this paper demands reverence and humility. We approach it with just that spirit and pray that God will illumine our hearts and minds, thus preserving us from wild and fanciful conjectures and reckless assertions that are without foundation. We feel about this subject as Robert G. Lee, a great preacher of the South, must have felt when he said: "I believe in recognition in Heaven as surely as I believe there is a God. If consciousness, character, love, memory, fellowship, are in that life, why should there be any question about it? May God help me for your sakes to take the doctrine of Heavenly Recognition out of the region of surmise and speculation into the region of absolute certainty."

Man is the acme of God's creation, the crown of all that our heavenly Father has brought into existence by His own mighty power. The remarkable strides that men have made in scientific research, in industrial progress, in agricultural development, and in the civilization and evangelization of the peoples of the world are an indication of the treasures of genius which God has put at man's disposal. Is it reasonable to believe "that He might lead it towards one place—a black hole in the ground where it could bury its intellect and memory and imagination and prayer in the depths with the leaf and the worm?" The answer is "No." If death means the utter forgetfulness of God-given gifts and of earthly friends and loved ones in the Lord, then this aching emptiness in our hearts never shall be satisfied, and the undying memory of departed loved ones will never be anything more than just a buried hope.

The Desire of All Nations

From time immemorial men have held to the doctrine of recognition in the future life. Like an unbroken thread in human history, there has been a deep conviction in man's spirit that the purpose of being created could not be fulfilled in his short-lived visit in this life.

The ancient Athenian philospher Socrates could say that since "death conveys us to those regions which are inhabited by the spirits of departed men, will it not be unspeakably happy to escape from the hands of mere nominal judges? Is it possible for you to look upon this as an unimportant journey? Is it nothing to converse with Orpheus, and Homer, and Hesiod? Believe me, I would cheerfully suffer many a death on condition of realizing such a privilege. With what pleasure could I leave the world, to hold communion with Palamedes, Ajax, and others!"

Cicero wrote: "For my own part, I feel myself transported with the most ardent impatience to join the society of my two departed friends. O, glorious day! when I shall retire from this slow and sordid scene, to assemble with the divine congregation of departed spirits; and not with those only whom I have just mentioned, but with my dear Cato, that best of sons and most valuable of men! . . . If I seemed to bear his death with fortitude, it was by no means that I did not most sensibly feel the loss I had sustained: It was because I supported myself with the consoling reflection that we could not long be separated."

Untaught savage kings in some part of the world believed that they could send secret messages to departed friends by whispering the message in the ear of one of their subjects and then immediately cutting off his head. It is reported that in some savage tribes, when a king died, hundreds of his subjects willingly submitted to death in order that their king might be better served in the spirit world. Even our American Indians, in some places, believed that when the tribal chief died, it was proper to slay his wife and other close associates in order that he might retain his dignity and be assisted by the same servants in the future life.

The belief in recognition and reunion in the after life is a universal one. It prevailed among cultured philosophers and poets, among untutored pagans, and it is voiced by the peoples of the world in our own day. The universal, instinctive belief is that we shall know each other in the future life. Someone has expressed the yearning of his heart in the following verse—

> "When the holy angels meet us
> As we join their happy band,
> We shall know the friends that greet us
> In that glorious spirit-land.
> We shall see the same eyes shining
> On us as in days of yore.
> We shall feel the dear arms twining
> Fondly, round us as before."

> Author unknown.

THE HYMNS OF THE CHURCH

For many years the Christian Church has been singing hymns that express positively the belief that heavenly recognition is a blessed assurance.

> "Oh, how sweet it will be in that beautiful land,
> So free from all sorrow and pain,
> With songs on our lips and with harps in our hands,
> To meet one another again,
> To meet one another again,
> With songs on our lips and with harps in our hands,
> To meet one another again."

"I'll soon be at home over there,
  For the end of my journey I see;
  Many dear to my heart, over there,
  Are watching and waiting for me.
  Over there, over there,
  I'll soon be at home over there,
  Over there, over there, over there,
  I'll soon be at home over there."

"I know I'm nearing the holy ranks
  Of friends and kindred dear,
  For I brush the dews on Jordan's banks,
  The Crossing must be near.
  O come, angel band, Come and around me stand;
  O bear me away on your snowy wings
   To my immortal home;
  O bear me away on your snowy wings
  To my immortal home."

"There's a land that is fairer than day,
  And by faith we can see it afar;
  For the Father waits over the way,
  To prepare us a dwelling-place there.
  In the sweet by and by,
  We shall meet on that beautiful shore;
  In the sweet by and by,
  We shall meet on that beautiful shore."

"When the mists have rolled in splendor
  From the beauty of the hills,
  And the sunlight falls in gladness
  On the river and the rills,
  We recall our Father's promise
  In the rainbow of the spray:
  We shall know each other better
  When the mists have rolled away.
  We shall come with joy and gladness,
  We shall gather round the throne;
  Face to face with those that love us,
  We shall know as we are known:
  And the songs of our redemption
  Shall resound thro' endless day
  When the shadows have departed,
  And the mists have rolled away.
  We shall know as we are known,

Nevermore to walk alone;
In the dawning of the morning
Of that bright and happy day,
We shall know each other better
When the mists have rolled away."

"Oh, the dear ones in glory, how they beckon me to come,
And our parting at the river I recall;
To the sweet vales of Eden they will sing my welcome home,
But I long to meet my Saviour first of all."

"Friends will be there I have loved long ago;
Joy like a river around me will flow;
Yet, just a smile from my Saviour, I know,
Will thro' the ages be glory for me."

"My loved ones in the Homeland
Are waiting me to come,
Where neither death nor sorrow
Invades their holy home."

HEAVENLY RECOGNITION IN THE OLD TESTAMENT

An encouraging oft-repeated refrain in the Old Testament substantiates the doctrine of Heavenly Recognition—

> "Then Abraham gave up the ghost, and died in a good old age, an old man, and full of years; *and was gathered to his people*" (Genesis 25:8).
>
> "And these are the years of the life of Ishmael, an hundred and thirty and seven years: and he gave up the ghost and died; *and was gathered unto his people*" (Genesis 25:17).
>
> "And Isaac gave up the ghost and died, *and was gathered unto his people,* being old and full of days: and his sons Esau and Jacob buried him" (Genesis 35:29).
>
> "And when Jacob had made an end of commanding his sons, he gathered up his feet into the bed, and yielded up the ghost, *and was gathered unto his people*" (Genesis 49:33).

"Aaron *shall be gathered unto his people*:
for he shall not enter into the land which I
have given unto the children of Israel, because
ye rebelled against my word at the waters of
Meribah" (Numbers 20:24).

"And the Lord said unto Moses, Get thee up
into this mount Abarim, and see the land which
I have given unto the children of Israel. And
when thou has seen it, thou also *shalt be
gathered unto thy people,* as Aaron thy brother
was gathered" (Numbers 27:12, 13).

When Abraham died, he was buried in a cave at
Machpelah in the land of his sojourn. He purchased
the field himself for a possession to be certain of a
burying place at death, but it was not the sepulchre
of his ancestors. Therefore, the language of Scripture
does not mean that his body was gathered to the place
of his forefathers, for some of them had died and
were buried back in Ur of the Chaldees. Notice also
that Abraham was gathered to his people before his
body was buried, for it was after he was gathered to
his people (verse 8) that his sons Isaac and Ishmael
buried him in the cave of Machpelah (verse 29). The
same is true also of Moses who was gathered to his
people, but whose body was buried in a valley in
Moab, and "no man knoweth of his sepulchre unto
this day" (Deuteronomy 34:6). As we study the lives
of other Old Testament characters of whom it is said
that they were gathered unto their people, we will
find that it meant more than merely being buried with
them. They were gathered to their loved ones in the
abode of departed spirits with not one moment's
solitude between their memories on earth and their
joining them in Heaven. A blessed recognition! A
hallowed reunion!

The attitude of David at the death of his child shows
that Israel's King believed in Heavenly recognition.

He had fasted and wept in the hope that God would be gracious to him and allow the child to live. But when final word was received that he was dead, David ate food, wiped the tears away from his eyes, and found comfort in a hope that he expressed in the words: "I shall go to him" (2 Samuel 12:23). Would there be any comfort for David if he had to go to his child whom he would not know? What would the blind get out of going to behold the sunset? What would the deaf get out of going to hear music?

May we say here that we do not believe there will be infants in Heaven as such. There will be no deformed, deficient, nor decrepit bodies in Heaven. There will be no old age or infancy in the home of the blessed. We have stated in the previous chapter that no infant who dies will be lost and sent to Hell. However they will not appear in their resurrected bodies as infants, for, as Dr. West has said: "Infancy is an immature stage and an imperfect state of existence. Adam and Eve were not infants when made, but adults." What a tragedy if weak and helpless infants are to be doomed to an eternal state of weakness and infirmity! We encounter no problem here in a parent recognizing its child in Heaven. When we think of Christian mothers who have died giving birth to a child, and the child growing to full maturity and becoming a Christian, we still believe that the mother shall recognize her son or daughter even though her last view of the child was in its infancy.

Heavenly Recognition in the New Testament

The scene on the Mount of Transfiguration is generally accepted as strong evidence of Heavenly Recognition. After death the spirit is clothed with a spirit body that is recognizable. This fact was in evidence when

Jesus took Peter, James, and John up into the Holy Mount. As Heaven shone forth in celestial effulgence, there appeared before Christ and His disciples Moses and Elijah. These two Old Testament saints did not appear as angels or ghosts, but, Luke says: "There talked with Him *two men*, which were Moses and Elias" (Luke 9:30). Not only were Moses and Elijah recognizable by our Lord, but they were known to the disciples also. Peter certainly knew them, for he said: "Jesus, Master, it is good for us to be here: and let us make three tabernacles: one for Thee, and one for Moses, and one for Elias" (verse 33). When we recall how the disciples with earthly, limited vision could recognize the two saints from Heaven, certainly when we arrive there in our glorified bodies and with heavenly vision, we will be able to recognize those with whom we associated on earth.

When the rich man died and went to Hell, "he lift up his eyes, being in torments, and *seeth* Abraham afar off, and Lazarus in his bosom." (Luke 16:23). Here is a case that proves both recognition and remembrance in the future life. If, in the abode of the lost with its limitations of spiritual wisdom and perception, there is feeling for and recognition of loved ones, how much greater will be the affinity and knowledge of our loved ones in the eternal Home of the redeemed where cognizance is not limited!

Heaven is revealed as a social place, where enjoyment and fellowship are set forth under the figure of a feast. Jesus said: "And I say unto you, That many shall come from the east and west, and shall sit down with Abraham, and Isaac, and Jacob, in the kingdom of heaven" (Matthew 8:11). Assuredly the patriarchs and prophets knew each other at this holy festival, and so will the saved from every quarter of the earth.

The Apostle Paul believed and taught that Heaven was a place of mutual recognition for the children of God. In his first Epistle to the Thessalonians, Paul wrote: "For what is our hope, or joy, or crown of rejoicing? Are not even ye in the presence of our Lord Jesus Christ at His coming? For ye are our glory and joy" (1 Thessalonians 2:19, 20). There is no mistaking what Paul had in mind. He fully expected to meet the converts from Thessalonica in Heaven, and furthermore, he looked forward to being able to distinguish them from others who had found Christ during the years of his ministry. By the Holy Spirit, Paul taught also that those who were saved under his teaching and preaching would know him. He says: "As also ye have acknowledged us in part, that we are your rejoicing, even as ye also are ours in the day of the Lord Jesus" (2 Corinthians 1:14). Elsewhere Paul speaks of "the whole family in heaven and earth" (Ephesians 3:15). Heaven is our home, and all who go there are one family with God as their Father. How sad if we had to live throughout eternity as strangers! It would not be home.

But we take courage and press on hopefully, "For now we see through a glass, darkly; but then face to face: now I know in part; but then shall I know even as also I am known" (1 Corinthians 13:12). Today our knowledge is confined to the revelation that God has given us, and how we do praise Him for that marvelous revelation in His Word! But in that day—"face to face"! O blessed hope! Face to face with family and friends whom we have loved and long since lost awhile. But more wonderful still: we shall see Him as He is, "face to face."

> "Face to face! O blissful moment!
> Face to face—to see and know;
> Face to face with my Redeemer,
> Jesus Christ Who loves me so."

INDEX OF SCRIPTURE TEXTS

121

BIBLIOGRAPHY

Barlow, J. L.—"Endless Being"

Candlish, Robert S.—"Life In a Risen Saviour"

Chafer, Lewis Sperry—"The Eternal Retribution of the Lost"
    Published by "Our Hope" July 1940

DeHaan, M. R.—"The Two Resurrections"

DeHaan, M. R.—"Resurrection and Heaven"

Dixon, A. C.—"The Modern Pulpit"   Sermon—November 1905

Graham, James R.—"Spirit, Soul and Body"

Grant, F. W.—"Facts and Theories as to a Future State"

Haldeman, I. M.—"Mortality or Immortality"

Harbaugh, H.—"The Heavenly Recognition"

Kimball, James William—"Heaven"

Kuyper, Abraham—"Asleep in Jesus"

Larkin, Clarence—"Rightly Dividing the Word"

Lee, Robert G.—"This Critical Hour"

Lockyer, Herbert—"The Immortality of Saints"

Morgan, G. Campbell—"The Teaching of Christ"

Peters, Madison C.—"After Death—What"

Rimmer, Harry—"The Evidences For Immortality"

Striker, William—"What Happens After Death!"

Thompson, Augustus C.—"The Better Land"

West, Anson—"The State of the Dead"

An Anonymous Author—"Heaven Our Home"